C000201586

GIBSIDE AND THE BOWES FAMILY

# Gibside and the Bowes Family

MARGARET WILLS

THE SOCIETY OF ANTIQUARIES
OF NEWCASTLE UPON TYNE
1995

Published for
THE SOCIETY OF ANTIQUARIES
OF NEWCASTLE UPON TYNE
The Black Gate, Newcastle upon Tyne
by
PHILLIMORE & CO. LTD.
Shopwyke Manor Barn, Chichester

© Dr. Margaret Wills, 1995

ISBN 0 85033 998 X

Designed by Henry Davy
Typeset, printed and bound in Great Britain by
Ward Colour Print
Gateshead

# Contents

# List of Illustrations

I would like to thank Alec Wills for his photographic record made of the many changes at Gibside since 1982 and for his help in the preparation of this book.

Sources are given in abbreviated form in brackets after each caption. These abbreviations are as follows:

AW Alec Wills
BL B. &. T. Langley, *Gothic Architecture Improved,* pl 39
BM Bowes Museum, Barnard Castle (Durham County Council)
CRCN City Repro, City of Newcastle
DRO Durham Record Office
GPL Gateshead Public Library
JF Jesse Foot, *The Lives of Andrew Robinson Bowes, Esq., and the Countess of Strathmore,* 1810. Frontispiece
JP James Paine, *Plans, Elevations, Sections I, 1767.* pls. 67-69. © University of Newcastle
JSP Post Card collection of J.S. Perry
MW Margaret Wills
NM Norman McCord, © University of Newcastle
SAN Society of Antiquaries of Newcastle upon Tyne
SE Strathmore Estates, Glamis; Newbery Smith Photography

# *Acknowledgements*

I would like to thank the following people for their help in writing *Gibside and the Bowes Family:*

Joan Auld, Harry Beamish, Greta Cairns, Ken and Sylvia Cheeseman, Dr. Eric Clavering, Jack Cowen, Ian Curry, Hugh Dixon, Peter Elphick, Dr. Constance Fraser, Ken and Joan Gardener, Dr. Peter Leach, Dr. Stafford Linsley, Dr. Hentie Louw, Dr. James Macaulay, Grace McCombie, Professor Norman McCord, Ralph Pattisson and Dr. Peter Willis.

The staff of the Local Collections in Newcastle Central Library and Gateshead Public Library have been most helpful. I would also like to thank the staff of the Record Offices I have used, in particular David Butler, Jennifer Gill and the staff at Durham Record Office where the greater part of the Strathmore Papers are housed. The owners and agents of country estates have been most helpful in enabling me to see buildings and landscapes to compare with those at Gibside, and I would like to thank them for making such expeditions memorable.

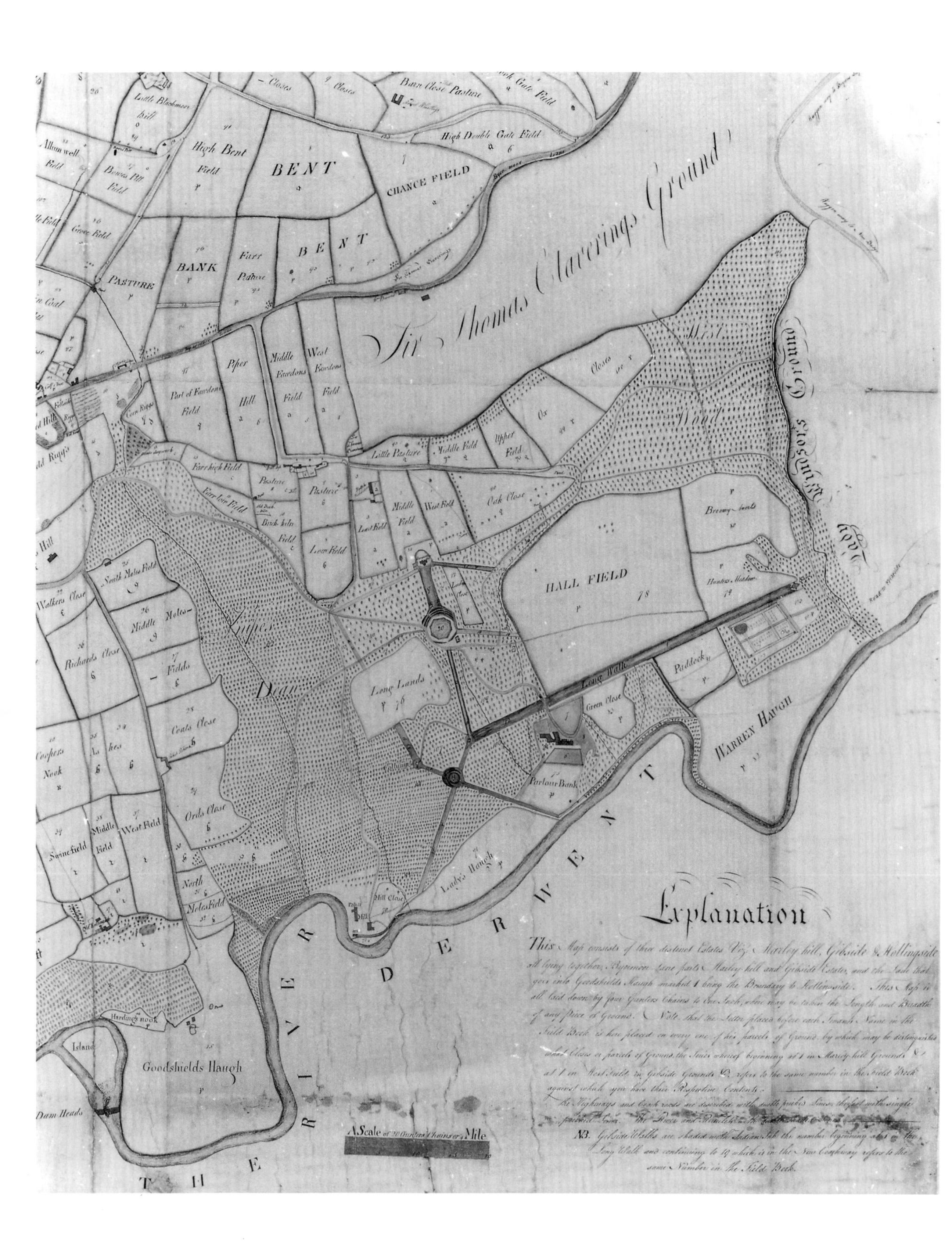

Little Blackmoor Hill
Allum well Field
Bowes Hill Field
High Bent Field
BENT
Barn Close Pasture
High Double Gate Field
CHANCE FIELD
Grove Field
BANK
PASTURE
Farr Pasture
B E N T
Sir Thomas Claverings Ground
Part of Fawdens Field
Piper Hill
Middle Fawdons Field
West Fawdons Field
Closes
West
Wood
Ox
Upper Field
Middle Field
Little Pasture
Farr high Field
Farr low Field
Pasture
Brick kiln Field
Low Field
Least Field
Middle Field
West Field
Oak Close
Broomy lands
HALL FIELD
Hunters Meadow
South Moles Field
Middle Moles Fields
Walkers Close
Richards Close
Snipes Dean
Long Lands
Long Walk
Paddock
Green Close
WARREN HAUGH
Coats Close
Coopers Nook
Ords Close
Parlour Bank
Swinefield
Middle Field
West Field
North Moles Field
Lady's Haugh
Mill Close
THE RIVER DERWENT
Hardings nook
Island
Goodshields Haugh
Dam Heads
A Scale of 20 Gunters Chains or 1 Mile
Explanation
This Map consists of three distinct Estates Viz. Marley hill, Gibside & Hollingside all lying together, Byermoor Lane parts Marley hill and Gibside Estates, and the Lane that goes into Goodshields Haugh marked 1 being the Boundary to Hollingside. This Map is all laid down by four Gunters Chains to One Inch, where may be taken the Length and Breadth of any Piece of Ground. Note that the Letter placed before each Tenants Name in the Field Book is here placed on every one of his parcels of Ground by which may be distinguished what Closes or parcels of Ground, the Series whereof beginning at 1 in Marley hill Grounds & at 1 in West Field in Gibside Grounds &c. refers to the same number in the Field Book against which you have their Respective Contents.
NB. Gibside Walks are shaded with Indian Ink the number beginning at 1 in the Long Walk and continuing to 19 which is in the New Coachway refers to the same Number in the Field Book.

Hawdon's field

# *Introduction*

The present-day approach to Gibside is by a steeply winding drive which leads to an enclosure by the Chapel House. Tall trees on one side and the walled garden on the other form a precinct to the unused graveyard. The Chapel was not designed to be approached from this angle, but by worshippers and visitors coming down the half mile long grass avenue. From there they could gradually appreciate the Chapel with its portico, dome and decorative detail.

This north west part of County Durham was an unlikely place to find such a Chapel. Gibside stands on the River Derwent and in its now tranquil valley an early Industrial Revolution took place.

Along the river in the eighteenth century were mills, forges and iron works, while coal brought the greatest profit. There was a forge and both bell-pits and drift mines in the grounds at Gibside, and although mining activities were kept as far as possible from the house, it was important as a source of revenue. At the beginning of the 18th century Gibside coal was considered to be the best to be found in London and it sold at a premium.

The early entrance to the Gibside estate was from the Whickham to Burnopfield road through the eastern part of the property. The drive led across fields, turned and then manoeuvred round a steep corner, where it was at one time near to a wagon-way carrying coals to the River Tyne. After more twists it reached Gibside House. The house stood at the edge of a platform above a steep drop to the water meadows at Lady Haugh.

Former owners of the estate were the Marleys, who held both Gibside and the adjoining Marley Hill nearly continously until 1540. The estate then became the property of the Blakistons through marriage and the Jacobean house was built by William and Jane Blakiston from 1603 to 1620. The three storey house was imposing with mullioned windows lighting the entrance rooms. Columns on either side of the porch supported small statues and the arms of King James I were carved over the door. There had been at least one previous house on the site, and inventories of its contents show that the fortunes of the Blakiston family had gradually increased.

The heiress to Gibside at the end of the seventeenth century was Elizabeth Blakiston who married Sir William Bowes at St. Mary's Church, Barnard Castle, on 17 August 1693. The Bowes family had lived at Streatlam Castle in the south of County Durham since early in the fourteenth century. They were active in policing the border between Scotland and England and gained preferment, and sometimes a knighthood, for these duties. Sir George Bowes was loyal to Queen Elizabeth I during the Rising in the North led by the Earls of Westmorland and Northumberland in 1569, and was rewarded with leases for lead mines. The family gained power and influence but by the seventeenth century the male line failed more than once, and the family fortunes were in danger of being dispersed.

William Bowes, great grandson of Sir George Bowes who had fought for the Queen in the Rising of the North, was born in 1656. He went to Trinity College, Cambridge in 1672 and was admitted to Gray's Inn in the same year. He was elected member of Parliament for County Durham five times in the period up to 1705. In 1674 he was knighted by Charles II at Whitehall, which may have been a purchased honour.

In the following year Sir William was made Chief Warden of all the King's Forest and Chases within the Lordship of Barnard Castle, Teesdale and Marwood. After his marriage to Elizabeth Blakiston a new period of prosperity began. Of their ten children four sons and four daughters survived infancy but their son John died of smallpox at the age of nine in 1714. Of the three remaining brothers two died in their early twenties, and it was the youngest, George Bowes, who became the owner of Gibside and the other Bowes' estates.

Map 1 (facing). Detail of plan of Marley Hill, Gibside and Hollingside Estates, copied from the original map by James Stephenson, 1767. North is at the foot of the plan.

CHAPTER

# 1

# *The Bowes Brothers*

Sir William Bowes' death in 1706 left his family of four sons and four daughters for Lady Bowes to rear. Sadly her youngest son John's death from smallpox in 1714 came four years before Lady Mary Wortley Montagu, a pioneer for inoculation, had her own son inoculated against the disease while living in Constantinople. Later inoculation became accepted in England as the best guard against the illness. However, Lady Bowes did not lack spirit, and took an active part in local affairs, including disputes over way-leaves and wagon-ways. William Cotesworth, the secretary of a local coal cartel, became her ally in 1712 when "at the pressing instance" of Lady Bowes of Gibside and in her company he assisted in pulling up a newly laid wagon-way over certain lands at Fawdonfield'[1] belonging to Sir John Clavering. She then retreated and left Cotesworth to bear the whole cost of the action.

She was determined to do her best for her children, and her eldest son, William Blakiston Bowes (born January 1st 1697) was first educated at the Grammar School at Durham under Mr. John Rymer, and then admitted to Trinity College, Cambridge. The Glamis record states 'He was a considerable traveller, and extensive collector of books. He seems to have suffered severely from constant ill health...' William had smallpox when in London in 1711[2] and afterwards was often unwell. He had an eruption of the face and hands which did not respond to treatment.

On the death of her father Sir Francis Blakiston in 1713, Lady Bowes was in charge of the Blakiston property until her eldest son came of age. In a letter from Durham of 10 July 1714 Dr John Bowes, Prebend of Durham, wrote to his sister-in-law of 'your son's recovery on his travels to Rome'.[3] William Blakiston Bowes set out again for France on 14 April 1715, and also visited Switzerland, Rome and Naples in 1716, engaging in the current fashion for the Grand Tour.

William was conscientious in visiting his younger brothers to see how their education was progressing. Thomas Bowes, the second son, had also been at school at Durham under John Rymer in 1712, and then both Thomas and George, the youngest surviving son, went to school in Newcastle in 1716. They were transferred to Mr. Hill's school in London in 1717, and it was there that William found them lacking in learning. He wrote to his mother from St. James's on 10 January 1718:

> I am oblig'd to tell you that Tommy is intirely resolved never to look on a Book... He also endeavours to pervert George, who advances much better, & I doubt not but will do very well, tho' it had been much to his advantage to have been separated from Tommy long agoe...

William Blakiston Bowes was a querulous correspondent. He complained about his mother not writing to him, and in January 1718 he queried her lack of haste in making a will, saying he was more likely to die in the near future than she. He was also anxious to add to their property, and wished to bid for the Harford Estate, which was to be sold in Chancery. If his mother wished to buy the estate, he would bid for it. He also wanted to buy property in the Durham area, and told his mother to buy Sellaby, near the River Tees, if she thought it advisable. In the same letter he wrote that his cold had gone 'but has been suceeded by a striking out in my Face & hands'. William was interested in coal mining techniques, and in a letter from St. James's of 13 March 1718 he wrote knowledgeably on the subject. He told his mother he did not wish to get involved in disputes over wagon-ways and wrote 'I am positively resolv'd never to meddle with it till you have made Your Jointure over to me'.[4] As this would in effect be making over at least part of her income to him it showed his greed and lack of consideration.

His mother was anxious for him to visit Gibside, but he refused, unless there were other attractions. He wrote from St. James's on March 20 1718:

> Surely you don't think me such a fool to prefer the Charms of a stupid, dull, Country Life, to the pleasure of the Town, & the

> addition of 1500£ per annum to my Estate, if You will find me any such advantagious proffer in Your Country, I will willingly set out to Morrow[5]

He was anxious to find an heiress for a bride, and was convinced he would have done so before, had it not been 'for that pestilential humour, that used every spring to strike out in my hands, & now has come out in my face with more violence than ever...'

He was still concerned with money matters, and upbraided his mother in the letter sent from St. James's on March 20th 1718:

> I had partly agreed to sell what we had in the South Sea at 19³/₄, but on your order would not stand to it, it is now fallen to 8 & will shortly be at par... for it is all your fault that we have lost above 500£.[6]

Perhaps in order to attract an heiress he started to rebuild the Bowes' family seat at Streatlam Castle. An agreement was made on 4 January 1717 between Samuel Burton for William Blakiston Bowes, and John Sands of Darlington for 1,000,000 bricks. From the accounts the greatest amount of quarrying and other building activity was from 1717-18 at the time of William Blakiston Bowes' majority. Sir William Bowes, an earlier owner of Streatlam, served twenty years in France and was knighted at Vernoyle in 1424. He had 'returned to England and rebuilt his mannor-place of Streatlam from the ground'.[7] The castle was rebuilt 'on a model sent from France'. William Blakiston Bowes started to rebuild Streatlam Castle incorporating part of the older building. William Fordyce wrote in his history of Durham published in 1857:

> The castle is three lofty stories in height, and 152 feet in length, which is less by 12 feet than the front of the former castle. Near the western extremity, the remains of a square tower are visible in the wall.... there was formerly a gateway, a moat, and a drawbridge.

Leaden spouts at Streatlam bore the dates 1717, 1720 and 1721. 'I have a house that is very near finished that will be the best in our Northern parts' wrote William Blakiston Bowes in 1720.

William was also anxious to add to the Bowes' estates, and wrote to his mother:

> I would have you let no opportunity slip of buying any Estate that is contiguous to Streatlam, High Lands, Kirk Leavington or Gibside; I am sure of it that You might have Red Hall Maynards, or Cowtons whenever you please, & at reasonable Rates.[8]

In the same letter he mentions that he is now of age, and wishes to marry. In his quest to marry an heiress he sought the help of Dr. James Jurin, a former master at the Royal Grammar School in Newcastle, who later took up a medical career, and supported Lady Mary Wortley Montagu in her crusade for inoculation against smallpox. Jurin was also a cousin of William Cotesworth, and would have known the background of the Bowes family well. Bowes made no effort to hide his mercenary motive in seeking a bride, and described part of his estate:

> at Lamesley I have a very good house and Gardens, fit for any gent. to live in. At Mickleton my Estate is 80 Miles Round... & very hopefull Lead Mines. I owe not one farthing in the World.[9]

He was seeking to marry a Miss Webster and the negotiations took some time. He wrote to Dr. Jurin from Gibside on 4 April 1721 that he was willing to go to London on a week's warning:

> if Sir Thomas approves my Estate, Person & Character, & can give with his Daughter 3000 £. on the Naill, & 3000 £. on the Birth of the 1st Child & 2000 £. more on that of the 2d. which I take to be pretty near equal to the 5000 £. demanded after Sir Godfrey's Death.[10]

Sir Godfrey had been another suitor for Miss Webster's hand and died while the negotiations were in progress. William had already asked Dr. Jurin to get a copy of the two grandfathers' wills to see how much the young lady had independent of her father. His plans came to nothing, and he wrote to Dr. Jurin on 3 May 1721:

> I am very well pleased the Young Lady is disposed of.... I was not in Love, for my Character is, je m'attache a la Sexe en general mais jamais en particuliere... all my Aim was Convenience...

and added that he would look for a young lady of

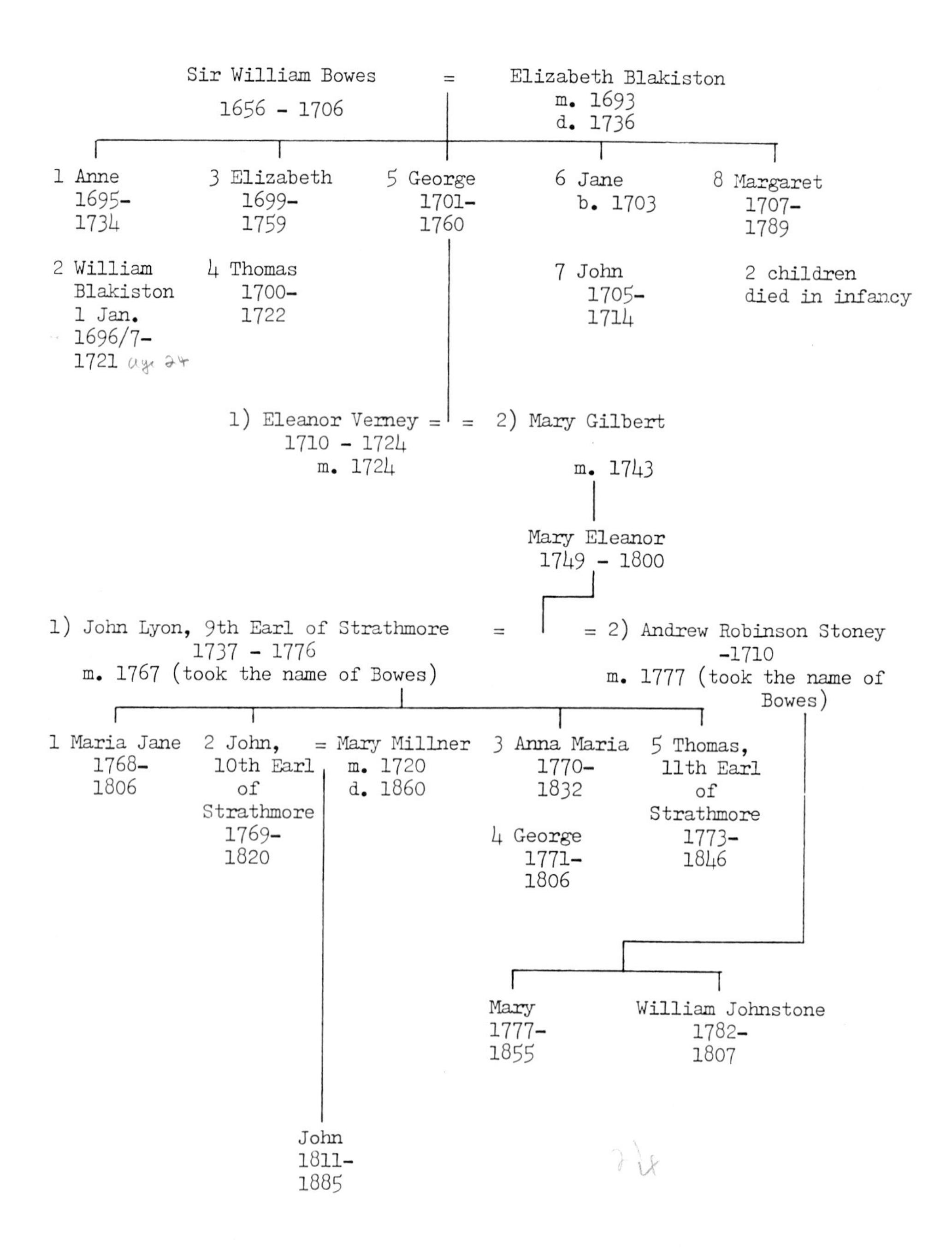


1. Pedigree of George Bowes and his descendants.

good fortune 'of a modest discreet behaviour not deformed'.

His interest was largely in business, and he wrote to Dr. Jurin from Gibside on 22 April 1721:

> last Monday we begun to lead the new Waggon Way, which is the beginning of my profitt; it is a work of such great importance, & crosses so many Mountains & Vales which are all levelled, that I can compare it to nothing more properly than to the Via Appia.[11]

In spite of all his efforts to find an heiress, and add to his fortunes by his business efforts, he died intestate, at the early age of twenty-four on 7 October 1721.

The second son Tommy had caused problems because of his inattention to school work, and his general lack of co-operation. William Blakiston Bowes had written to his mother of Tommy that he was 'impatient to be gone from School, & is daily quarrelling with Mr. and Mrs. Hill', who ran the school in London which Tommy and George attended. Tommy had asked his elder brother to write to Lady Bowes saying he wished to be apprenticed to a merchant. William thought he would leave before his time was out 'by reason of his uneasy temper, which does not suffer him to agree with anybody'. Tommy did not enter trade, but was appointed an ensign in Peacocks Regiment on 22 January 1719. He died suddenly, apparently of a fit, at Kensington and was buried there in 1722. Thus George Bowes, following the death of his two elder brothers, became the possessor of Gibside and the other Bowes' estates in the same year as he attained his majority.

CHAPTER
2

## GEORGE BOWES 1701-1760

# *The Count*

### *Bowes as a Young Man*

George Bowes in his twenties can best be described in a poem entitled 'An Enquiry after a Northern Member supposed to be Lost or Miss-Layd at the Last Masquerade', which may refer to Bowes first standing for Morpeth and then Durham County in the Parliamentary election of 1727:

> He's about six foot in Height,
> Wo[ul]d he walk but upright...
> His complexion is good...
> His Mouth & Nose small...
> His Eyes grey as a cat
> Hansom Legs, Autre Chose,
> And his Name is George Bowes.[1]

His daughter referred to him as 'uncommonly handsome', and the painting of him, now at Glamis Castle, shows a broad, oval face, long nose, and the pose of a man used to authority. He is shown with his helmet and sword, a reference both to his early life in the army, and perhaps to his involvement on the side of George II to forestall the second Jacobite uprising. The portrait was by Enoch Seeman, a court painter, and the portrait is recorded in the Gibside Journals in 1745 when they 'Paid Mr. Isaac Seeman for a picture of Mr. Bowes by the late Enoch Seeman in full of all accounts £10 10s'.

He had looks, personality, and a talent for business affairs. He was also overbearing and autocratic, with the rashness of youth. His fiery temper led to a duel in 1726 between him and one of the coal-owning Clavering family. It is not clear who was his opponent, but it is most likely to have been James Clavering of Greencroft, nicknamed 'Vaudois'. The family seat was at Axwell Park two miles down the Derwent valley from Gibside. Bowes lacked tact and James Clavering was an exceedingly quarrelsome man, who had spent a year in jail for threatening his brother-in-law with murder. He was twice Bowes' age and if he was the opponent he managed simply to wound Bowes in the arm, according to the ethics of duelling, and to avoid a fatality.[2] His dealings over the coal trade showed that as well as possessing business talent, he could be an awkward and skilled adversary in negotiations. His life was not all business, however. His daughter referred to him as 'a great rake in his youth' and one of his partners, Edward Wortley Montagu, wrote from Newcastle to his wife in July 1729:

> We hear no news here but of the gaietys of my two partners, Sir H. Liddel and Mr. Bowes, who are so much taken up with feasting and balls that I have had a good deal of difficulty to get them to settle to business.[3]

He accepted his position as the head of the Bowes family with its responsibilities, and was an active participant in local affairs. He was chosen as Alderman of Hartlepool in 1729 becoming its Mayor in 1732 and in the same year contributed to the building of the harbour pier. As the cost of holding the office was in excess of any income derived from it, his motive must have been to secure and keep voters in that part of his parliamentary borough. He was elected Mayor of Hartlepool for a second time in 1743 and again in 1754. This latest selection as Mayor coincided with his re-election to Parliament in 1754 and support from the Hartlepool voters would have helped in his return to Parliament. He was elected Mayor of Durham in 1732, 1738 and 1753. Before his last term as Mayor Bowes refurbished Durham Guildhall in 1752, and the panelling in the Mayor's Chamber bears the Bowes' coat of arms. Bowes became a member of Parliament for the County of Durham in 1727 and was returned as member until his death in 1760. He was made Collector of Customs at Bridlington in 1730. The salary for such a post was small and although he bought properties in North Yorkshire, the post was outside his parliamentary constituency. He spoke against Walpole's Excise Bill in 1733 on one of the minor points: 'Mr. Bows *(sic)* answered him, and they say well,

2. Portrait of George Bowes, by Enoch Seeman, 1744.

considering he is a young speaker.'[4] Bowes was an active lobbyist on behalf of the coal trade and aimed to be in the House of Commons when such subjects were discussed.

His acts of public generosity were largely connected with electioneering, and are meticulously entered in the Gibside Journals and Cash Accounts. Under the heading 'By Accot. of Election for County of Durham' the Cash Accounts record in 1729: 'Paid Philip Donnison & John Kent Church Wardens 20 Gns. Subscribed by George Bowes Esqr. towards a set of Bells for Gateshead Church' £21. Another set of bells was given in July 1746: 'By Election for County. Paid Sunderland Church-wardens George Bowes Esqurs. Subscription towards a Sett of Bells' £30. He also paid a subscription to Durham Races as part of the same election campaign. He made gifts to the city of Newcastle by subscribing to the Free School, or Grammar School, there from 1739 onwards.[5] His efforts to become a freeman of Newcastle were finally rejected in 1741, but this did not prevent him from making a yearly subscription of £50 towards the building of the Infirmary in Newcastle, and giving a further £100 in 1752,[6] when the Palladian hospital on the Forth Banks to the West of the town was nearly complete. His interest was also practical for the architect of the Infirmary was Daniel Garrett, who had worked for Bowes, and the hospital grounds were laid out by William Joyce who made the walks at Gibside.[7] At the anniversary meeting of this charity on 27 June 1753, George Bowes was one of the six presidents of subscribers, together with the Earl of Northumberland, the Earl of Tankerville, Lord Ravensworth, Sir Walter Blackett, and Henry Partis, Esq., Mayor of Newcastle.

A more personal gift indicative of Bowes' taste was that of two handsome silver flagons presented to Whickham Church and engraved 'Ex dono Georgii Bowes, Armiger. Anno Domini 1722'. They were given in the year in which Bowes inherited Gibside. His connection with Hartlepool, before he became its mayor, was marked by the gift to St. Hilda's Church of a baluster font in Yorkshire marble with his name and the date 1728 carved on its base. Bowes had inherited the Streatlam stud from his father, and in 1753 he won the first royal purse of 100 guineas on the Town Moor Newcastle upon Tyne, with his bay horse Cato. To commemorate victory he presented the town with his prize to buy a piece of plate. As the money was given to the town it need not necessarily have been his choice, and the plate, with heavy filagree edging, was engraved with the King's arms, those of the town, and of Bowes. The salver became the trophy for the Northumberland Plate, known locally as the 'Pitmens' Derby'.

George Bowes was interested in the arts and strove to acquire knowledge while at Gibside. In August 1736 he paid Isaac Thompson a 'Subscription to his Course of Philosophy £5 5s', and later subscribed to the Society for the Encouragement of Learning in London. In February 1745 the Accounts record 'Paid for Popes Essay on Man and a qur. of paper'. He subscribed to three architectural books which were to be influential, William Kent's *The Designs of Inigo Jones* (1727), James Gibbs' *Book of Architecture* (1728) and Isaac Ware's edition of Palladio's *The Four Books of Architecture* (1738).

He was concerned with his family, and kept in touch with his first wife's mother for over forty years. Their excursions were enjoyable and he kept a record of one in 'an Acct. of the Charge of Geo Bowes Esq., going down the water with the Honbl Mrs Verney at the Fort.

5th September 1734.

| | |
|---|---|
| To 10 bottles of Wine | £1: 0: 0 |
| Bear | 0: 10: 0 |
| Porter | 0: 1: 6 |
| Brandy | 0: 1: 0 |
| Bread | 0: 2: 6 |
| Empty bottles | 0: 0: 9 |
| Trouble of the house | 0: 6: 3 |
| The Sergant by my Mastrs Order | 0: 5: 0 |
| Oyle of Roses | 0: 0: 6 |
| Bottle for the Musicks | 1: 8: 0 |
| Barge | 3: 5: 0 |
| | 7: 0: 6 |
| Recd. from Geo Bowes Esq | 5: 5: 0 |
| | £1: 15: 6[8] |

It is not explained whether the amount remaining was discount, or to be paid later.

Bowes' friendships were with those of similar interests. Thomas Robinson (1700-1777), of Rokeby, Yorkshire, made Bowes' acquaintance in 1724 when they both wished to enter Parliament. They had a mutual interest in architecture, and as a follower of Richard Boyle, 3rd Earl of Burlington (1694-1753), the arbiter of Palladian taste, he may well have introduced Bowes to Kent's *The Designs of Inigo Jones* (1727), which was published from drawings in the collection of Lord Burlington. Robinson may have influenced Bowes in his choice of Daniel Garrett (active 1727-1753) as the first architect known to have been employed at Gibside. Garrett was Robinson's protégé and was recommended to his family, friends and acquaintances. The 3rd Earl of Carlisle, the builder of Castle Howard, later became Robinson's father-in-law, and Robinson was his chief architectural adviser after the deaths of Vanbrugh, Hawksmoor and Etty, the creators of Castle Howard.

Another friend with a keen eye for building was Sir Hugh Smithson, later to become Earl, then Duke, of Northumberland. Smithson became Garrett's second patron in the north, and is thought to have employed him at his seat Stanwick Park, north Yorkshire. The Vanes of Raby Castle, near Streatlam, were other well-known patrons of Garrett, and friends of George Bowes who was godfather to Raby Vane (1736-1779).[9] Unfortunately this friendship was ended by a dispute over rival claims to some common land to the west of Streatlam, which led to a protracted lawsuit in which George Bowes lost his case.

As well as a keen interest in architecture George Bowes loved music. Two German boys who played the waldhorn lived at Gibside for three years and amused the company. Music was no doubt one of the accomplishments of the Tinkler Row Strollers, the Whickham Strollers and the Strollers from Bryans-Leap, who entertained Christmas gatherings at Gibside. While in London in 1731 he hired a harpsichord for five months, and wished to play the violin. This was the favourite instrument of Charles Avison (*c.* 1710-1770) the renowned organist of St. Nicholas' Church, Newcastle, who may well have been his tutor. Bowes subscribed in 1739 to concerts given by Avison, at the cost of a guinea, and paid Mr. Avison 'for some paper to Write Musick'.[10] While staying in London he visited the opera, and in 1745 paid a first subscription of ten guineas for a winter season of three operas. On 9 March 1745 he 'Paid at Garricks benefit 5s.' and later in the month he visited Ranelagh, the fashionable pleasure gardens at Chelsea.

Bowes had a passion for horses, and enjoyed foxhunting and horse-racing. He owned and bred race-horses and maintained the Streatlam stud. He attended local race meetings, and visited friends in Northumberland to go fox-hunting. He was also keen on playing cards, and had a Missasippy table for gaming at Gibside[11] and also one at Ledston, a house that he rented and used as a staging-post on his journeys to London.

As many of the younger sons of the gentry had done before him Bowes joined the army, and became a captain in General Wade's regiment. His daughter in her *Confessions* wrote that 'when only eighteen he ran away, and laid out money his mother had given him for other purposes, in buying a commission in the army, where he continued until he came to the estate.' On inheriting Gibside in 1722 he no longer needed a commission. This was sought after by a certain Benjamin Smith, who sent a letter to Captain Bowes at Gibside on 22 February 1722. He wrote 'I am informed of your desire to dispose of your Commission in General Wade's Regmt. of Horse', and wanted to know if the commission were for sale, its correct price, and asked for a reply by return of post.[12] Later in the year the matter seemed settled, as George Liddell, a neighbouring coal-owner, wrote to William Cotesworth:

> Mr. Bowes I hear is Expected home tomorrow. His man Mills says the Errand he went to London upon was to dispose of his Commission, which by reason of his absence they designed to have filled up.[13]

William Blakiston Bowes had shown a great interest in the coal industry, and had been trained for it, but this was cut short by his early death in October 1721. Like his elder brother George Bowes wished to exploit coal deposits on his estate and nearby, and also hoped that

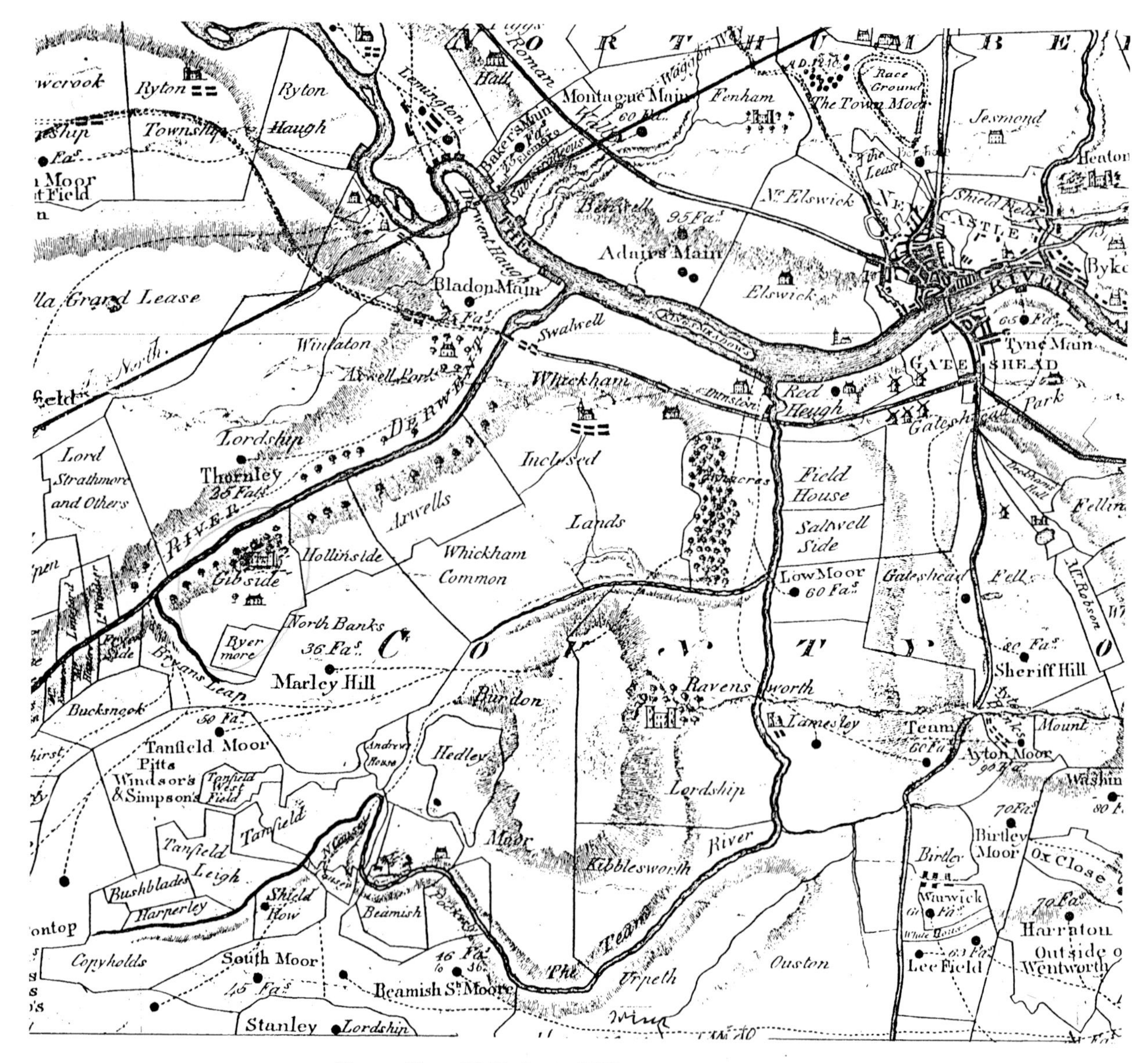


Map 2 Map of Collieries, by William Casson, 1801, detail.

further iron deposits might be found at Gibside. A clerk in the Secretary of State's Office, also called George Bowes, wrote to his namesake of iron mines about Gibside and 'Mr. Woods scheem for your Iron works for pig Iron and Malleable Iron & the Queen wore a Rose in her breast of this Iron'.[14] He continued that it was by forging iron in Sir Ralph Blakiston's time 'that the family raised themselves by those works in the Infancy of the Coale'. It was true that there were deposits of both lead and iron in the Derwent Valley, as well as coal, but they were not easily exploitable. The river itself was a source of energy, and its swift currents provided opportunities for the use of water-power. There had been both fulling and corn mills on the Gibside estate, and the corn mill was converted to a paper mill in 1728. The River Derwent, which bordered Gibside to the west, not only gave a source of power, but was a picturesque boundary to the estate.

It was coal, however, that was to be the source

of George Bowes' wealth. Ever since Lady Bowes had left William Cotesworth to bear the cost of uprooting the wagon-way through Sir John Clavering's land at Fawdonfield in 1712, there had been bad feeling about the matter. When Bowes gained control of Gibside he saw way-leaves as profitable and objected to a new wagon-way passing through his land without a revised leasing agreement. He held that as a copy-holder he could obstruct the building of the wagon-way, even if the other copy-holders consented. He said that if the proposed line went ahead he would pull it up. His dispute with William Cotesworth was largely due to this disagreement. Bowes' fiery temper led him to threaten Cotesworth who wrote to Lady Bowes on 5 July 1721 'he seems to threaten to take away my life by unlawfull means...with many Repeated abuses & affronts'.[15] Later in his letter he complained that 'threats to take away my Life are continuous acts of outrage not heard of in the Country since I have Lived'. In the end Bowes had to pay the full cost of the actions against him in a case brought by Cotesworth on 12 March 1723. Cotesworth wrote to his friend George Edwards of young Bowes:

> I met him since when he complained I Lost him his Election at Berwick. I told him I was not sorry for it tho' I was not the occasion for it.

Cotesworth wrote to his steward Thomas Sisson after the judgement that Bowes 'is to pull down his foolish hedge & to Remove the Rubbish – wee moved to have him stand Convicted & pay our Costs...'

This seems to have had little effect however, as George Liddell recounted when he wrote from his brother's home at Ravensworth Castle to William Cotesworth, on 17 March 1723:

> Mat. Bell show'd me yours to him yesterday, & tells me that if the Count does not remove the hedge, your people are to do it, & set on your waggons to morrow.

Liddell mentioned reports that Bowes had departed for Berwick, where he hoped to stand for Parliament, and continued:

> I should be pleased if it were true, for I think him a very improper man to be trusted with our Liberty & propertys. I doubt he will prove full as bad a Neighbour as his Bror. If he gets a share of Dawsons & Claverings Colliereys he wil be past dealing with.

George Bowes' high-handed ways in business matters earned him the nickname of 'Count'. William Cotesworth's son Robert referred to him as 'Csar' in a later letter. The picture is of an arrogant and strong willed man, all the more determined to get his own way because of his extreme youth, and who would stop at nothing to get what he desired – at least in business

As well as taking on the management of his family's dealings in the coal trade, Bowes wanted to enter Parliament. It had been a tradition for some time for the head of the Bowes' family to be in Parliament, for it led to power in the county. As the coal trade was the basis of Bowes' prosperity, and also an important factor in the fortunes of Durham County, it was a great advantage to have influential coal-owners to speak and lobby in the House of Commons. Bowes had hoped to enter Parliament as the member for Berwick in 1723, but his dispute with Cotesworth overshadowed the attempt, and the matter had to be postponed.

Bowes decided to marry. It was to be a marriage of considerable wealth and influence. Discussions about the marriage took place as early as 1720, when Eleanor Verney, the bride-to-be, was only ten. In a letter from John Rudd of Durham concerning the marriage settlement it was reported that Eleanor would come into the sum of £15,000 if she married after the age of fourteen. The wedding took place when she attained that age. The bride's father, the Honourable Thomas Verney, died of smallpox in 1710 and Eleanor became the sole heiress of her grandfather George, Lord Willoughby de Broke, Dean of Windsor, and Registrar of the Order of the Garter. The family seat was at Compton Verney, but Eleanor lived in Whitton, situated between Windsor and Isleworth. The latter had her grandfather as patron of the living. She was beautiful, learned, and very young at the time of their marriage. In a letter to her of 20 July 1724 George Bowes wrote:

> I am not able to bear the cruel absence from my Angel any longer without haveing recourse to Pen & Paper for relief of my

> tortured Heart which can at present find no other way to ease its self[16]

and they were married on 1 October 1724. Perhaps to welcome his new bride an arch was put up in the garden at Streatlam, the work being carried out from July to August of that year. Their marriage appears to have been one of affection, but there was also a marriage contract with due provision for a marriage settlement. When Eleanor died after only two and a half months of marriage, George Bowes had to pay back the settlement, with interest added. The Gibside Journals record:

> Lord Willoughby. Debtor to Proffit and Loss £15000 for so much as my Wife's Fortune in his Lordship's hands as she dyed without issue the [14th] day of December 1724. I was married 1st October proxime and said Fortune is payable with Interest from marriage £15000.[17]

The interest on the sum for a year at 5% was £750.

Bowes was overcome with grief. In a letter to his mother sent from London on 28 January 1725 he wrote:

> My Dear Girls death had taught me by experience what I before only thought, that this World is a continued Scene of Misfortunes.[18]

Eleanor Bowes' early death prompted Lady Mary Wortley Montagu to write her epitaph coloured by her own rather jaundiced view of marriage. The poem began:

> Hail happy bride, for thou art truly blest!
> Three months of rapture, crown'd with endless rest.[19]

The poem was widely circulated and much copied.

Bowes' sorrow lasted for several years, according to his letters, and he threw himself into dealings with the coal trade. He pleaded ignorance of such matters, but drove a hard bargain in spite of what he said. George Liddell wrote to William Cotesworth on 22 March 1725 of a meeting with Bowes:

> I was yesterday at Gibside from Eleven till five, & not a Soul besides. We talked a great deale, but did little. He is desirous of an agreemt. with you & us, but sayes Mr. Wortleys must be content with a Small proportion of any new Colliereys. He would have us draw a Scheme for he had not a head for it he sayes.[20]

It is evident from the tone of the letter that although George Bowes was only twenty-three (born 21 August 1701) he understood negotiations well, and was ready to grasp any advantage.

On 17 June 1725 George Liddell, George Bowes and Charles Atkinson met at Mr. Hodshon's in the Flesh Market, Newcastle upon Tyne. They proposed a regulation of the coal trade and listed likely participants, with the areas they controlled. The following April an agreement was signed between George Bowes and William Cotesworth for a 51 year term. They agreed to drop all suits against each other, and not to promote suits by third parties in which either of them were involved. They also came to an agreement on the way-leave over Whickham Fell, which had been a cause of dispute for years. This agreement led to a larger settlement between the Wortleys, Liddells, Bowes and Cotesworth, which was agreed in the Summer of 1726. This was the origin of the 'Grand Alliance'. It was similar to the agreement between George Bowes and Cotesworth, save the new partnership was for 99 years. They also agreed to have mutual use and maintenance of wagon-ways, and to work 'agreed' quantities at the partnership collieries. The whole enterprise had to be worked as a joint concern, with consultation over buying new leases on collieries or way-leaves. This powerful partnership dominated the local coal trade, and was probably the most important association of coal owners in the eighteenth century.

## *The Building of Causey Arch*

This partnership led to George Bowes' first architectural venture, that of building a bridge to carry a wagon-way over the Causey Burn, three miles to the south-east of Gibside House. In August 1725 Ralph Wood, a local stonemason, began to build what became known as the Causey Arch, the first railway bridge of a large single span in the world. The building of the bridge was itemised in 'George Bowes Coal Accounts with Liddell and others' which were kept from 26 August 1725 to 11 June 1726. George Bowes was responsible to the Trustees of Sir H. Liddell Barnt., George Liddell Esq., and the Honble. Sidney and Edwd. Wortley Esq., and Thomas Ord Esq. Bowes appears to have been the co-ordinator of the building of the bridge, and certainly kept the accounts for it. The sum spent was £2454 19s 5d. Bowes' share of the cost was £731 13s 1d. The cost of stabling added another £30, while the cost of the inspection of the bridge was extra. The final accounts were signed by 'a quadruple alliance' on 1 May 1727

G. Bowes
G. Liddell
Thos. Ord
Robert Cotesworth.[21]

Some sixty years later an anonymous journal writer was impressed by the bridge:

> on my return to Newcastle I passed over Tanfield Bridge (commonly called Causey Bridge) a structure the most awful and magnificent my Eyes ever beheld, it consists of one single Arch 178 feet High and 102 feet wide, thrown over a deep Glen whose steep sides are covered with a rich luxuriancy of wood watered at the bottom by a rapid rivulet.[22]

Bowes pursued his aim to become a member of Parliament. Almost as soon as he withdrew from the Berwick election of 1723 he planned to stand for a seat at Morpeth. In December 1723 the Gibside Ledgers record 'By the Morpeth Election £2913 4s. 11d.' Thomas Robinson was also mentioned in the Ledgers in October 1724, though he cannot yet have been involved in the Morpeth contest. The Morpeth seat was under the patronage of the Earl of Carlisle. The votes were cast by the Morpeth freemen, but their number was controlled by the Earl as he could restrict the admission of new freemen. His son, Lord Morpeth, had been returned to the two previous Parliaments without the expense of electioneering, in return Lord Carlisle let the corporation arrange the second seat as they wished. George Bowes took advantage of this situation, by-passed the corporation, and gained a majority of the voters by promising them £20 each. Bowes deposited £1000 as a guarantee that the freemen would be paid. He was so successful in his tactics that when he withdrew to contest Durham County, two days before the election, some voters still voted for him, and not the substitute candidate, Thomas Robinson.[23] Thomas Robinson's debt of 50 guineas was increased by £1100, which was the amount recorded in the Gibside Ledgers on 31 December 1727 as 'To Morpeth Election'. At the same time the Journals record:

> Morpeth Election
> debr. to Jane Wharton of Gilling
> Wood £1200
> For so much Borrowed on Geo. Bowes Esqr. and Sir Thomas Robinson's Bond This Money was sent to Ainsley Donkin at Morpeth to give among the Freemen there.

This is followed by an entry to Sir Thomas Robinson for £1100. He gave two bonds for this amount to George Bowes.

Bowes was successful in gaining a seat in Parliament for Durham County, the county where both Gibside and Streatlam were situated, as well as most of his properties. He had devoted a great deal of his time to the election, and once in a position of some power could hope to have an influence in coal trade matters. At that time Parliament met every year for five or six months, usually beginning in November or December. Bowes was now committed to spend part of his time in London to attend Parliament, but with the pattern of his life more settled, he must have felt able to do more than merely maintain Gibside. He could now improve his property and plan a layout which would show his estate to the best advantage.

CHAPTER
# 3
# *This Retired Place*

## *Early works at Gibside*

Before George Bowes began to plan the layout of his estate, he had to remove the settlement that had grown up to the east of Gibside House in order to serve the property and its mines. In a map of 1712, showing the route of the wagonway which caused the dispute with Cotesworth, the village at Gibside appears to be as large as Whickham[1]. These dwellings stood in the way of Bowes' improvements and their removal may have taken place either when he inherited, or after Bowes' failure to enter Parliament in 1723.

In the year George Bowes first entered Parliament he sought advice from William Etty (*c.* 1675-1734) of York as to the layout of the estate at Gibside. Etty combined the functions of carpenter, carver and architect. He laid out the grounds at Temple Newsam House, near Leeds, for the 4th Viscount Irwin in 1712, and was Clerk of Works for Colen Campbell (1676-1729) at Baldersby Park (formerly Newby Park) in 1720-1. He then worked for Sir John Vanbrugh (1664-1726) as Clerk of Works at Seaton Delaval from 1719 onwards, and at Castle Howard from 1721. He also supervised the building of the Mausoleum there, designed by Hawksmoor (*c.* 1661-1736). He was a man of experience in both building and landscape gardening and wrote to George Bowes from York:

> York, the 17th June 1727
>
> Honoured Sir,
>
> I have sent yr Honor a Single Plan of the House, and An Other Generall Plan with the House Stables and Principall Court and Avennew as allsoe the Out Lines of the Wall and Bastions, which should be don in such alike manner, which may Be further thought on: When surveying more exactly: I have sent Two designs for the front, and One for the Stables with its inner courting as you may see in the General Plan: I shal be mighty Glad to hear your aprobation: these Being the first Thoughts.
>
> I wish your Honr. Good Health.
> and Long life
>
> I am
> Your Honrs Most
> Humble Servant
> To Command
> Will: Etty
>
> Post Script
> The Box with the drawings coms in the Stage Coach and will be in London on the Tuesday the 20 instant.[2]

The letter was addressed to George Bowes at Mr. Dawson's Chambers, Gray's Inn, Holborn, London. Unfortunately these drawings are now lost, but Etty must have considered the estate as a whole and provided designs for a house and avenue with a series of walls and bastions. The latter were perhaps similar to those at Castle Howard where he was clerk of works. There is a reference to his work in the Gibside Estate Journals of 25 March 1727. 'Paid and Given Mr. Etty of Yorke for his trouble & Journey in drawing a Plan of the house & Garden of Gibside' £10 10s. Judging from Etty's letter they were preliminary plans, which could be altered as desired, and would have to be surveyed more exactly if they were to be carried out. As there were no further payments to Etty it looks as if George Bowes considered the plans, but decided not to implement them.

Bowes was now spending part of his time in London to attend to Parliamentary and other business, and his steward felt he was neglecting his estate. He wrote from Gibside recommending that 25 decaying trees should be cut down in 'the West Wood & also taking down all ye decaying trees in Snipe's Dean'. In March 1729 his steward complained: 'The Gardener is at a loss for the Trees you promised to send down, he says if they are not Shipt, but done immediately, they may yet come in season.' New woodlands were added to the estate at this time, and in June 1729 the Estate Journals record 'cutting 6000 sodds to the new walks in the new plantations', while in the following year 37,500 quicksets were planted in the avenues at Gibside.

During the first years as owner of Gibside House, Bowes maintained the fabric, added fourteen sash windows, and moved the kitchen, stables and other offices from the west end of the house to the east. If his marriage to Eleanor Verney had been longer lasting he might have been able to afford to build a new house, for she was the sole heiress of her grandfather, Lord Willoughby de Broke. As it was Daniel Garrett may have produced a plan for a new house based on Palladian principles, but it was never executed. Bowes' income fluctuated with the coal trade, and was too committed to undertake a substantial building programme on a grand scale. He adminstered his mother's jointure, and his three sister's incomes, and in fact acted as their banker. Anne, his eldest sister had married Edward Chaloner of Guisbrough in 1713, when Bowes was still a boy. His youngest sister Margaret later married Thomas Liddell, the brother of their near neighbour at Gibside, Henry Liddell of Ravensworth Castle. His sisters Elizabeth and Jane did not marry. He was able to use their money to finance his enterprises as long as they had their allowances to live on. His greatest outlay was in buying adjoining land to increase his estates, or properties where coal or lead might be mined. He did however have enough money to finance small buildings or landscape improvements at Gibside. These were largely undertaken by estate labour aided by skilled craftsmen who worked on the estate, with specialists called in to provide expertise and give decorative finish. The construction of these buildings was usually spread over five or more years, with the main attentions focussed on one building at a time.

## *Switzer's Plan for Gibside*

In November 1731 another plan for the grounds of Gibside was put foward by Stephen Switzer (1682-1745), but as this plan and those of the following year do not survive the extent of his involvement in the layout is conjectural:

> By Garden Charges. Paid Geo. Bowes Esq., he paid Mr. Switzer for drawg. a Plann of Gardens, Plantations, Green Close &c. £10[3]

Bowes, in accordance with his policy of making payments personally to artists and craftsmen who made a particular contribution to the estate, met Switzer on this occasion.

Stephen Switzer was an important figure in the history of English landscape design, and flourished in the transitional period between the formal garden and the informal landscape. After an apprenticeship with George London (active *c.* 1675-1714) he helped to lay out the grounds at Castle Howard, and in particular Wray Wood where straight paths linked circular open spaces with a statue or other conceit. In 1705 he went to Blenheim and worked with Henry Wise (1653-1738) and John Vanbrugh, where he was concerned in canalizing the River Glyme, and digging the foundations of Vanbrugh's bridge over it. He published *The Nobleman, Gentleman, and Gardener's Recreation* in 1715, the first volume of his most famous work, which he published in three volumes in 1718 as *Ichnographia Rustica.* He set up as a seedsman in London in 1724, and combined this with writing about landscape design while continuing to practice. He held that a whole estate should be the subject of a design, which should be accomplished by one or two great axial lines, linking the house and estate in the grand manner. He favoured circuits round an estate with ha-has to enhance the view, and water as an element in design. The rest of the estate should be laid out with regard to good sense, the type of land found, the trees it bore and its agricultural improvement.[4] The fact that Switzer was called in at Gibside was in line with George Bowes' practice of getting the best possible advice and relying on it when it suited his own ideas.

A further payment was made to Switzer on 8 August 1732 when he was paid £5 10s for trees. On the same day William Leaton, the Gibside agent, noted that £35 had been borrowed from Switzer, which was repaid shortly afterwards on 28 August. When the loan was repaid he was given £3 for his trouble, together with 4 guineas for further plans, for unlike William Etty he had been asked to develop his ideas. As no other payments to Switzer are recorded the work must have been carried out by estate labour, and without Switzer's supervision. The payment for trees at the beginning of August shows Switzer in his role as nurseryman.

Switzer worked at Park House, Gateshead, for Henry Ellison, William Cotesworth's son-in-law. They corresponded for at least two years, when

Switzer contrived to get Ellison's gardener Wooley dismissed in 1733 for cheating his master, and then tried to find a replacement. Switzer also did business with Bowes' neighbour Sir Henry Liddell of Ravensworth Castle. Sir Henry had another house in the country at Eslington, Northumberland, which had been rebuilt by 1730. The site was low-lying with a diminutive River Aln flowing past. A large oval basin was made before the house and the river dammed to form a lake. Gardens and a broad terrace walk were made south of the lake where there was more land available and it is probable that the terrace, basin and general composition were by Switzer.[5] There is no known connection between Switzer and Wallington, Northumberland, but there is circumstantial evidence that Switzer may have prepared one of the two surviving early designs for the grounds at Wallington. Switzer's work in the north east of England has not yet been fully investigated, but he undertook work in the Gateshead area, and in all probability worked in Northumberland during the early 1730s.

Switzer's first plan for Gibside included the gardens, plantations, Green Close and other parts of the estate, and gave the general layout which was followed by Bowes in the years to come. Straight walks and rides, which were still preferred by many clients, were laid out near the house, and a circuit including a walk engineered on the River Derwent's banks, was begun a month after Switzer's second plans for Gibside. James Stephenson's plan of Marley Hill, Gibside and Hollinside estates of 1767 shows that the area near the house had a very different layout from the rest of the estate. Here the straight walks and rides contrast with the haphazard line of field boundaries and lanes. Subsidiary paths were more sinuous, but the general layout was precise and formed the basis of the nineteen 'Gibside Walks' shown on Stephenson's map. Switzer's planned walks focussed on such features as a small round basin, which was terraced above in his characteristic manner, while from there another walk led off at right angles to the River Derwent. The most impressive part of Switzer's scheme was the octagon basin with its amphitheatre-like ramps in three stages above it where classical statues were later displayed.[6] From there a wide *allée* led upwards to a platform, which was to be the site of a future building, and made a bastion-like projection into the surrounding arable land. The projection was divided from the fields by an extended ha-ha, one of Switzer's favourite devices. He sought by this means to lay open the surrounding countryside to view and to extend the apparent size of the estate by removing its boundaries. Dézallier D'Argenville (1680-1765) had been the first to describe the ha-ha in his book *La Théorie et la pratique du jardinage* (1709) and it was used initially in England by Charles Bridgeman (1709-1738), though Switzer did not acknowledge this when he described and illustrated a ha-ha in *Ichnographia Rustica*. In his description of a ha-ha he wrote that it was 'by the *French* call'd l*a Fossé*, from the *Latin*, *Fossa*, *a* Pit' and the term fosse was used to describe the invisible boundary in the records of estate work at Gibside. It was not until 1755 that the term 'ha-ha' occasionally appeared in the accounts. Switzer's landscapes needed to be planned ahead, and he designed economically for the best use of land for the production of trees as well as amenity. The carrying out of his plans was a long term commitment, and by the time that the Grand Walk was made in 1746-9 it was beginning to look old-fashioned. By then the influence of William Kent (?1685-1748) meant that curved lines and walks were in vogue.

Shortly after Switzer's second plans for Gibside, the work at 'building a bridge at the new walk up Darwen Side' was begun.[7] The walk was engineered partly by making a shelf across a steep slope while the bridge crossed one of the two narrow denes. The bridge, which crossed the gill near the site of the future Bath House, was carefully constructed, and the bed of the stream under it was paved with stones to make it stable, before the water fell in a sheer drop to the River Derwent. Work continued on the high and low walks near the Derwent for a year, and on 15 September 1733 the first mention of the Bath House was made in the Cash Accounts when payment was made for 'Wallers &ca at the Bath'.

Map 3 Gibside Estate and its buildings. OS map 1862.

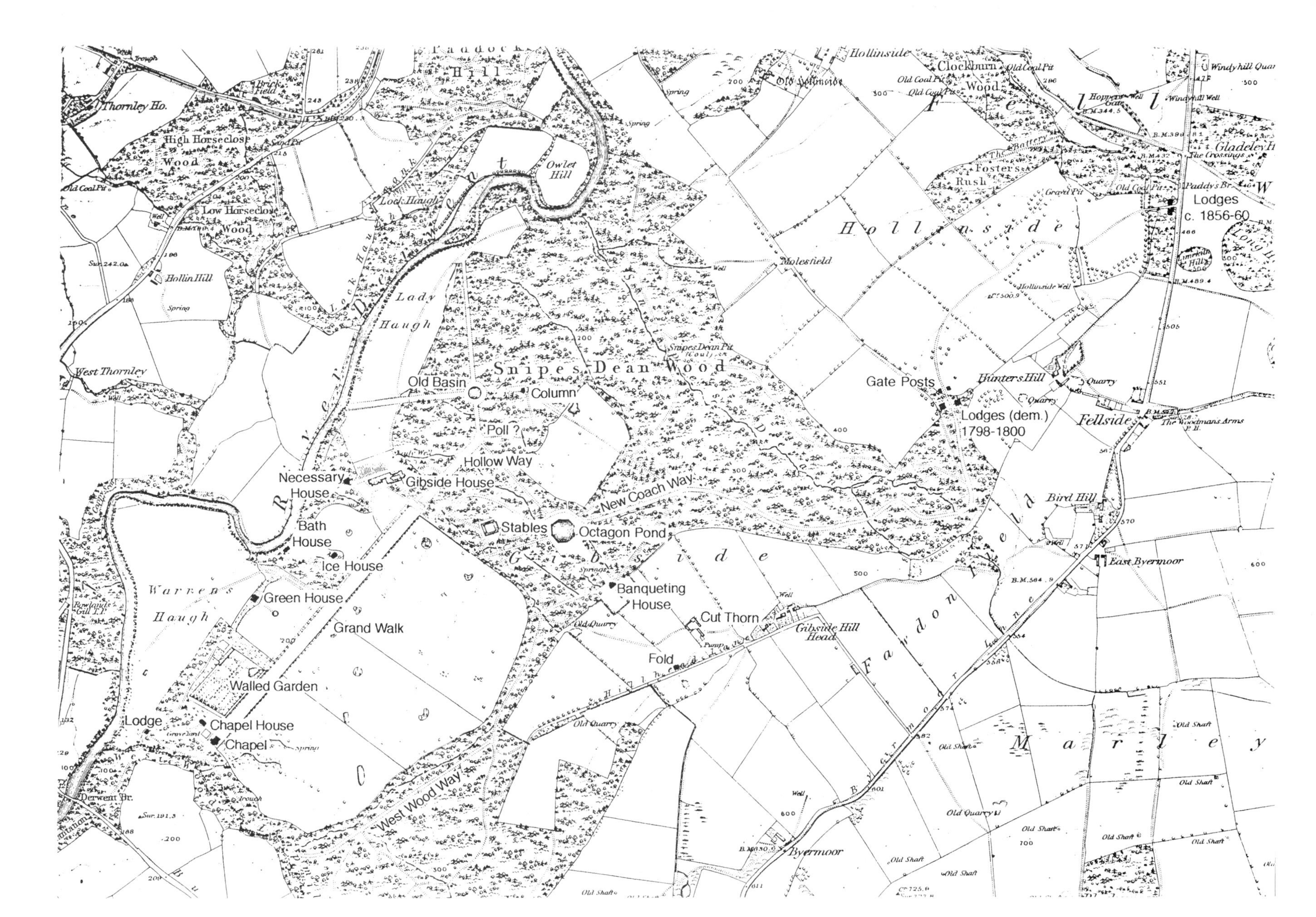
Thornley Ho.
High Horseclose Wood
Low Horseclose Wood
Hollin Hill
West Thornley
Owlet Hill
Lady Haugh
Snipes Dean Wood
Old Basin
Column
Poll ?
Hollow Way
Necessary House
Gibside House
Bath House
Ice House
Stables
Octagon Pond
New Coach Way
Warrens Haugh
Green House
Grand Walk
Banqueting House
Cut Thorn
Fold
Walled Garden
Lodge
Chapel House
Chapel
Derwent Br.
West Wood Way
Gibside
Gibside Hill Head
Fardon Field
Byermoor
East Byermoor
Bird Hill
Marley
Hollinside
Molesfield
Gate Posts
Hunters Hill
Lodges (dem.)
1798-1800
Fellside
The Woodmans Arms
Clockburn Wood
Fosters Rush
Lodges
c. 1856-60
Paddys Br.
Gladeley
The Crossings
Windyhill Well
Hollinside Well
Snipes Dean Pit
Old Quarry
Old Shaft
Old Coal Pit
Spring
Well
Quarry

## *The Bath House*

It is significant that George Bowes' first venture into architecture on his estate was to build a bath house. He followed the example of Lord Burlington, who returned from the Grand Tour and designed and built a bath house in the grounds of his Jacobean house at Chiswick in 1717. This *bagnio* was called by Colen Campbell in the third volume of *Vitruvius Britannicus* (1725) 'the first Essay of his Lordship's happy Invention'. We have seen that through his friendship with Thomas Robinson, Bowes may have been introduced to Burlington's work, and two of the books to which Bowes subscribed were published under the architect-earl's aegis. These books must have helped to form Bowes' taste for Palladian architecture. Bath houses or bathing rooms had been built from time to time in the seventeenth century. Edzell Castle, Angus, a tower house dating from the first half of the sixteenth century, had a summer-house and bath house built on to it in 1604. John Aubrey, in his *Brief Lives*, wrote that there were two 'bathing rooms' in the lodge built by Francis Bacon at Verulam, near St. Albans, in the early 17th century. Dr. Oliver of Bath, in his influential treatise *A Practical Dissertation on the Bath Waters* (1707), recommended cold baths as an aid to health. Although the cold bath had no medicinal effect, both public and private baths were built, and were held to alleviate all manner of ills. They became meeting places, and in the case of private bath houses, more particularly a male preserve. Baths were not taken regularly, but perhaps once a week, or once a month, with servants carrying water to the bath if a constant water supply was not available. Unlike Lord Burlington at Chiswick, or George Doddington at Eastbury Park, Dorset, Bowes did not choose a two storey bath house. His was a simple classical one-storey building consisting of three rooms with a portico in antis, and a room leading from the portico on either side. The small room behind the portico was used as dressing room and all three rooms had fireplaces.[8] The rooms flanking the portico had sash windows with stone surrounds. There were triglyphs below the pediment and quoins accented the corners of the building. The Bath House was approximately 47 ft. x 15 ft. 6 in.

Bailey's view of Gibside in 1782 shows the Bath House as a very small building on a low level, compared with the not yet castellated Gibside House. A clearing marks the site of the Bath house today, and it is due to Martha Helen Davidson, a distant cousin of John Bowes, George Bowes' great-grandson, that we have a record of it. She stayed with Lady Maria Jessop, George Bowes' grand-daughter, at Bird Hill on the Gibside Estate in 1827, and her drawings formed the basis for the Gibside Sketch Book. The drawings were competent, with a certain charm.[9] She showed the drama of the large drop between the Bath house and the River Derwent below, and revealed that by 1827 its roof had vanished. Her careful drawing showed that the Bath House stood above a sixty foot cliff, partly retained by stone blocks, with a balustrade to protect the path in front of the Bath. Her oblique view showed the Bath with a dramatically placed tree, and a wall of stone blocks flanking the balustrade.

Without her help it would be impossible to find a prototype for the Bath House, but comparing her drawing with the building shown on the right of plate 84 of James Gibbs' *Book of Architecture* (1728) gives a possible model, and it is from one of the three books on architecture to which we know George Bowes subscribed. The Bath House at Gibside appears to be a faithful copy of what Gibbs termed 'Two Draughts of a Building for the Menagery at *Hackwood*... That with the Columns is built'. George Bowes also preferred the building with columns. James Gibbs (1682-1754) was born near Aberdeen, and intended for the priesthood. Disliking the strict regime at the seminary he attended in Rome he became a pupil of Carlo Fontana (1638-1714), then the leading Roman architect. Skilled in draughtsmanship he made drawings for the visiting nobility and gentry. He returned to England in 1709 with a thorough training in architecture and became one of the most successful architects of the day. He made alterations to Park House, Gateshead, for Henry Ellison about 1730. He published three books on architecture which were influential and his *Book of Architecture* (1728) was one of the most used pattern books of the time.

3. Conjectural plan of Bath House, based on survey of surviving foundations.

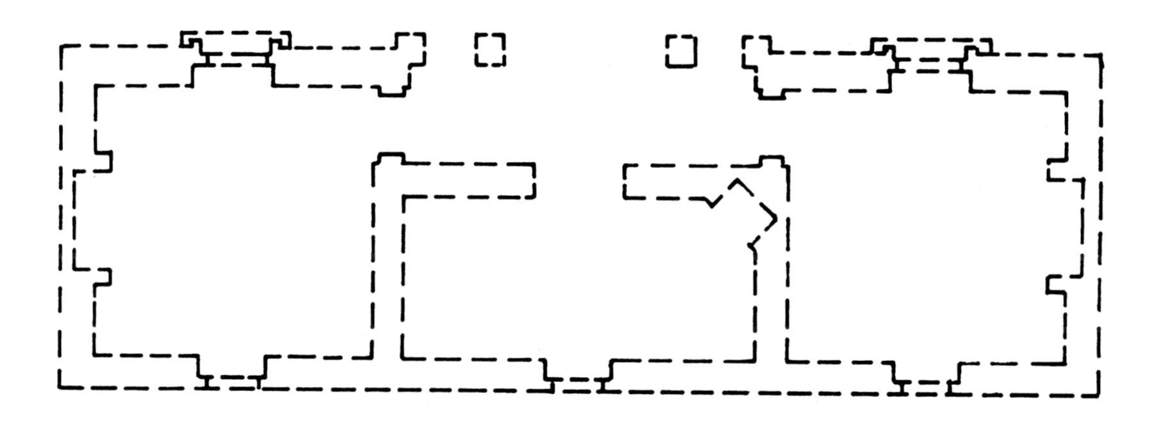

The front part of the Menagerie at Hackwood had the same shape and main disposition of elements as the Bath House at Gibside, though the Menagerie originally had two additional rooms with a separate entrance behind, and a staircase to the upper floor. The measurements of the two buildings were also similar. In Martha Helen's drawings of the Gibside Bath House the roof had disappeared, but the gaunt gable at one end must have supported a pitched roof, with a shallow pitched roof joining it to the pediment, as can now be seen at Hackwood. The Bath was part of the development of walks along the bank of the River Derwent, which was later to be known as Lady Walk. The path led from the west end of Gibside House and followed a broad curve to the river bank. It then led downstream to join a ride focussed on the small round basin, later referred to in the records as the 'Old Bason'. An alternative path followed the Derwent upstream, crossing two gills high above the river. The cliff above sedimentary rocks was retained by stone blocks clamped by irons, with drainage holes at intervals.[10]

The Bath House had been first mentioned in the records in September 1733. By November of that year Joseph Palliser, a carpenter and one of the skilled estate workers, was paid for roofing the Bath, and the following May made sashes for it. In October 1734 Palliser paid 'for a piece of

Leather for the Plug at the Bath', and by November Jon Bickerdike was 'wainscotting and flooring several rooms at the Bath'. Two months later Samuel Clark was 'putting up a Marble Chimney and Fixing Iron Rails Round the Bath', and the Bath House was nearing completion.

The decoration of the Bath did not follow the usual sequence where a plasterer worked before the floorboards and wooden wainscoting were in place. The first payment for plasterwork was made in October 1734 and payments continued for eighteen months. Francesco Vassalli (active 1715-1763) was commissioned to do the work. He was a Swiss stucco worker, born at Riva St. Vitale near Lugano. His first recorded work in England was at Duncombe Park, Yorkshire, about 1715. Later he worked at the now destroyed Sutton Scarsdale, Derbyshire, where rich plasterwork was carried out in collaboration with Adelbertus Artari in 1724. He also worked at Ditchley House, Oxfordshire, which was designed by James Gibbs. Here he collaborated with both Giuseppe and Adelbertus Artari and Francesco Serena.[11] The rich Baroque stuccowork round the door leading from the entrance hall to the saloon, was itemized in a bill submitted by Vassalli in 1725 on behalf of himself and his partners. They charged £21 'for doing the six Images over the pediments'. The sumptuous plasterwork was continued in the saloon, but Gibbs was also trying out the new Palladian idea of symmetrically arranged panels and decoration on the walls. Vassalli decorated the hall and five other rooms at Aske Hall near Richmond, Yorkshire in 1730, which unfortunately have not survived, while he and his assistant Martino Quadri decorated the Great Hall at Towneley Hall, Burnley, Lancashire in 1730-1. The Great Hall had been created by Richard Towneley in 1725-30 by doubling the depth of the former great hall, while it remained two storeys high. Grooved pilasters framed medallions containing Roman Emperors' heads, while clusters of fruit and cherubs were depicted in coving above the tall entablature. In the parlour at Towneley Hall Vassalli and his assistant worked on a smaller scale, decorating the fireplace in high relief. Vassalli's name has been linked with the Garter Room at Lumley Castle, a short distance from Gibside. This may be because medallions with the heads of Roman emperors, motifs often used by Vassalli, were part of the decoration, but these could also have been used by other stuccoists. Pietro Francini (active 1730-60?) is thought to have been responsible for the plaster-work at Lumley Castle and he worked for Sir Walter Calverley Blackett at Wallington, Northumberland. Here Daniel Garrett created a suite of three reception rooms about 1739, from what had before been the entrance front of the house. Francini decorated these rooms with elaborate Baroque plasterwork and some low relief ribbon-work. The first payment to Francini for this was in 1740 six years after the first payment to Vassalli for his work on the Bath House. Unfortunately as the Bath House was destroyed by a landslip in the middle of the nineteenth century we have no record of the form the decoration took, though some comparison as to the cost of the decoration can be made with work done at Towneley Hall. For the rich stuccowork at Towneley Hall Vassalli was paid £126 for the Great Hall, and a further £21 for the staircase.[12] He was paid just over £140 for his work at the Bath House at Gibside, which indicates that the stucco work in the three small rooms must have been rich and elaborate. It was a considerable payment for his work at that time. He was paid £20 in October 1734, and a further £30 the following April. The largest payment was made at the end of 1736, and was for work done early in the year:

> Garden charges Debr. to
> Francis Vassally £70 12
> for Stokoe Work done at the Bath
> as pr. Account on ye File 10th Feby. 1736.
> N.B. The agreement was for 100£ but he allow'd 29£ 8 for several things he did not finish.[13]

A further entry was made in February 1737: 'By Fra Vassalli 10° Feb. Paid him in Full as P. Account' £20.12.–. Whether the contract was not fulfilled because Vassalli was a careful workman and had not had time to complete his task, or whether he was erratic in his work cannot be established from the records. The last mention of Vassalli in the Cash Accounts is for August 1740 when he was paid 15s. 'for White Washing the Rooms at the Bath'. Why he should have returned to Gibside to undertake such a mundane task is not clear, especially as after finishing the plasterwork at the Bath he went on to design the stuccowork at Vanbrugh's Temple of the Four Winds at Castle Howard, and carry out the commission for the 3rd Earl of Carlisle there from 1737-9.

The scale of the Temple of the Four Winds was similar to that of the Gibside Bath House, which perhaps led to some affinity between the two schemes of decoration. What is certain is that there were statues at the Gibside Bath as there were at the Temple at Castle Howard, because in February 1739 Joseph Palliser was paid for 'taking down Venus at the Bath and making trows' (i.e. troughs) 10s. 8d, and in August 1763 his account was for 'setting up the Statues at the Bath and Painting them'. The Bath was completed in 1736, and as well as housing the cold bath it was a place to retire and play cards. The Gibside Inventory of 1743, made when George Bowes married his second wife, gives details of furniture suitable for relaxation and card playing, including 'a fine Inlaid Walnut Tree Card Table'.[14] By the time a new Inventory was made in 1746 a few items of furniture had been removed, and the little back room was referred to as the 'Little dressing Room at the Bath'. The Bath appears to have been kept in repair until 1804, but by the time Martha Helen sketched the building in 1827 the roof had already fallen in. Later when the Bath was engulfed by a landslip, the stones were taken and used for cottages on the estate.

The architect of the Bath House is not known. William Etty's connection with the estate had been in 1727, and his plans rejected. Stephen Switzer had submitted plans for the Gibside Estate in 1731 and the following year, but the design of specific buildings was not mentioned in the records. The first payment to Daniel Garrett was made in November 1740 when the Bath House was complete and is likely to be connected with later work. The plan of the building was simple, enhanced by the rich decoration in stucco by Francesco Vassalli. The Bath House was the first of the buildings built by Bowes to surprise and delight visitors in their walks at Gibside.

## *The New Walled Garden*

While the Bath house and its approaches were constructed, other work on the estate was carried out. The walled garden was moved from its position near Gibside House to a site some 500 yards to the south west of it. It became customary to have a kitchen garden some distance from the house so that the noxious smells of night soil and manure used for its cultivation would be less noticeable. Work began on the walled garden in 1734, when the bricklayer, William Dodgson, undertook to finish the wall by that summer. By June 1735 coping stones were added to the wall, and doors were fitted. A basin was made in one corner, there were also hot beds, and espaliards were added round the walls. Dodgson pointed the garden walls in June 1736 and his work was complete.

A new bowling green was constructed, and first mentioned in the records in 1733. The fact that John Stokoe was paid in January 1734 for 'twenty seven days Leading with his Wain Sods to the New Bowelling *(sic)* Green and Stones to the Garden Wall foundation' may mean that the bowling green was sited on the square of land near the walled garden, which later became the graveyard for George Bowes' chapel.

As improvements were made to his estate George Bowes wished to show them to his friends. A memorable event in 1736 was the visit to Gibside of the 3rd Duke of Cleveland and his wife. The Duke's grandmother had been a mistress of Charles II who granted her the title Duchess of Cleveland. The Duke's sister had married into the Vane family of Raby Castle, which provided a link with the area. The Duke owned a house at Hartlepool where George Bowes had been Mayor and benefactor, while Bowes was on friendly terms with the Vanes. It was a busy time at Gibside and the labourers were taken from their usual work in the gardens to help in the stables during the visit. The company sailed down the Tyne in a barge to Tynemouth accompanied by a Custom House boat and a Towns boat, with gunners to escort them.

4. The Walled Garden.

### *Bowes' New Properties*

As well as constructing new buildings at Gibside, Bowes had acquired more property. Negotiations to buy Stocksfield Hall had been begun by his eldest brother in 1720. Bowes completed the deal in 1730 at the cost of £2,800 and an annuity for the owner, which was to devolve upon his son. He bought the Lordship of High Worsall, near Yarm in the North Riding of Yorkshire. The price was £14,300, a considerable sum for that time, but it was worth it to Bowes because it was suitable for hunting. The land was bordered by the River Tees and its steep banks resembled part of the Derwent River. The Shield Row purchase of July 1734 was made for business reasons. It included a colliery and was four miles to the south east of Gibside. The purchase price, shared with two other coal magnates, was £3,000 of which Bowes paid £1000.[15] He also owned salt-pans, ships and gradually added to his Account of Jewels, which had reached over £3,272 by 1725 after his first wife's death. Thus George Bowes bought property and valuables, paid his legal advisers a small proportion of what he owed them each year and manipulated his fortune to his advantage.

### *The Hollinside Purchase*

An opportunity to improve the approach to Gibside House arose in 1735 when Bowes acquired the neighbouring estate of Hollinside. He wrote to Mrs. Verney, the mother of his dead wife:

> I have this day purchased at the expense of £10,000 my neighbour Harding's estate, which I have long wished for, as it will not only greatly enlarge my possession at this retired place, but will give me room to make new beauties by its happy situation, which afforded no delight to the owner, who had been loaded with lawsuits ever since he was in possession of it.[16]

Part of the agreement was that Bowes would pay Ralph Harding senior an annuity of £100, and his eldest son Richard £80 a year, and settlements were made for other members of the family.[17] This property to the north east of Gibside included a fortified manor house, parts of which dated from the thirteenth century, some colliery works, arable land and woods. It gave Bowes the opportunity to change the rather awkward approach to Gibside House, and to follow Addison's precept that 'True Happiness is of a retired Nature, and an enemy to Pomp and Noise... It loves Shade and Solitude, and naturally haunts Groves and Fountains, Fields and Meadows'.

In this essay on possessions and pleasure as opposed to happiness, which appeared in *The Spectator* of 17 March 1711, Addison longed for rural retirement. This had been a theme of poets since its praises were sung by Virgil and Horace. Following this tradition Edmund Spenser wrote idylls of the countryside, while Milton sought 'retired leisure' in *Il Penseroso,* and in *Comus* 'Wisdom's self oft seeks to sweet retired solitude'. In a more practical vein George London and Henry Wise published their translation of Louis Liger's gardeners manual plus some other works as *The Retir'd Gardn'r* (1706). This desire for a rural retreat was linked to the *beatus ille* concept that man was happiest when he renounced pleasure, riches and honour, and spent his life contemplating the wonders of nature.[18]

Bowes had a classical education, and must have been familiar with the idea of a longing for a country retreat expressed in poetry and prose. His brother William Blakiston Bowes had been a keen book collector, and in September 1730 two cartloads of books and pictures were brought from Streatlam Castle to Gibside. The library at Gibside House already existed, and was plastered in readiness to house the books. The catalogue of 'Books at Gibside' made in 1793,[19] contained works of Spenser, Milton and Pope as well as books on architecture, language and philosophy. There were also books on gardening, such as Sir William Temple's works, with his early essay on gardening (1685), and Philip Miller's *Gardener's Dictionary,* which was one of the most influential books on the subject in the 1730s. Bowes must have been familiar with a great number of the books given in the 1793 catalogue, and they must have influenced his attitude to his estate and its improvement. His ideas about Gibside were summed up in the letter to Mrs. Verney when he wrote to her about the Hollinside purchase. His use of the phrase 'retired place' to describe Gibside showed that he was well acquainted with the frequent use of the adjective in the literature of that time. Few of Bowes' letters survive, and it is in those to Mrs. Verney, his friend and confidant for over forty years, that he was most expansive over the plans for his estate. With the purchase of Hollinside Bowes could plan an easy access from Fellside Road to the north-east of Gibside House. The old road had a number of right angled turns with rather a steep hill, while the new drive curved through Hollinside Park before entering Gibside woods, and then dropped more steeply through Snipes Dene Wood towards the mansion.

## *The New Coach Way*

The New Coach Way was begun in 1738 and its construction took two years. It was made by estate workers, and the man in charge was William Joyce (active 1730-1767). Joyce joined the estate in 1730 and became head gardener there in 1734, when he was paid the yearly salary of £40. He was allotted a room in Gibside House as a valued member of the staff. He was probably the originator of the 1735 plan for the grounds at Wallington, Northumberland, made for Sir Walter Blackett.[20] The estimate for the plan, made in 1737, was certainly his. According to his wife's obituary he 'was first surveyor of the

Durham turnpike road, and the principal director of the much-admired walks and gardening at Gibside'.[21] Joyce combined this with becoming a seedsman specialising in growing trees. Bowes was pleased with his work on the new drive, for in November 1739 a payment of £21 was made to 'William Joyce as Gratuity for giving directions, and attendance on making the New Coach Way'.[22]

Bowes had acquired the land he wished to perfect his estate, and had made a new and more impressive approach to his house. He could now devote his energies to make new delights among the trees and denes of Gibside.

CHAPTER

# 4

# *'Its happy situation'*

## *Buildings on the Approach to Gibside House*

The New Coach Way descended for a mile through woods before Gibside House was reached. Bowes wished to 'make a pretty Landskip of his own possessions', and enhance the approach with buildings for delight and use. A small basin already existed where the rides from the river walk and the Long or Dove Cote Walk met. The New Basin was begun in July 1740[1] and was situated to the south of a curve in the New Coach Way, opposite the pasture known as Long Lands. It was octagonal, perhaps following Batty Langley, who in his *New Principles of Gardening* (1728) wrote of 'an *octagon Basin of Water* which may be adorn'd with Neptune'. This book was dedicated 'To the Nobility and Gentry of Great Britain' whom Langley hoped to have as clients. His forward-thinking ideas were tempered by those of the previous age, so that patrons used to formal gardens would not be discouraged.

## *Octagon basin*

The New Basin may have been octagonal in emulation of the larger octagon lake at Stowe. This had been constructed as part of Bridgeman's plan for Stowe, and was seen by Lord Perceval on a visit in 1724. Bowes, together with Mrs. Verney and Lady Stewart Shirley, visited Stowe in September 1737,[2] he must therefore have seen the octagon lake and been impressed by the walks, water, monuments, and also the rides joined by curving paths in the far plantations. By

5. The Octagon Basin.

January 1741 the estate labourers were working 'at the New Bason and Walk from it to the Old Bason'. This part of the development of Gibside was based on the plans submitted by Stephen Switzer in 1731 and 1732. On a platform overlooking the octagon pond a belvedere was planned backed by a scoop of land to the south east and a foss to divide it from the fields. Below the platform was banking and then a wide walk fell steeply to the New Basin. Directly above the New Basin was an amphitheatre-like structure which resembled the amphitheatre at Claremont, Surrey, but on a much smaller scale.[3] The walk then continued as a narrow ride until it met paths to the Old Basin and the Long Walk. The New Coach Way, with its sinuous curves, had not been part of Switzer's plan for Gibside, for the land to make this approach possible was not acquired until 1735.

## *The Gothick Building*

As the architect for his new building Bowes chose Daniel Garrett. Garrett was one of Lord Burlington's architectural assistants who often acted for him as clerk of works. In 1727, with the help of Lord Burlington, Garrett became Labourer in Trust at Richmond New Park Lodge, a subordinate position in the Office of Works. He was dismissed from this post ten years later for neglecting his duties.[4] At the time of his dismissal he was building up an architectural practice in the north of England helped by Sir Thomas Robinson. Sir Thomas recommended Garrett to a wide circle, and wrote to his father-in-law, the Third Earl of Carlisle, in March 1738 that he was:

> extremely glad Mr. Garret's designs meets *(sic)* with your approbation. I have since introduced him to Lord Derby, for whom he has drawn some plans, and who is also greatly pleased with his works... In short, all those who[m] I have recommended Mr. Garret to, have thanked me for doing it.[5]

Garrett is rather a shadowy figure, and Robert Morris (*c.* 1702-1754) dedicated a plate in *Rural Architecture* (1750) to him as 'the facetious Mr. Daniel Garrett', and wished that he might be rid of care and the pains of gout.

Garrett crossed swords with a relative of Robert, Roger Morris (1695-1749), over his designs for Cleveland House in London. Here Morris had exceeded his brief, changed the plans, and overspent.[6] Garrett's pithy comment on a correctly drawn column, compared with that designed by Morris, was 'Vitruvius Says if any One alter this he is a great Block head'.

On the recommendation of Sir Thomas Robinson, Garrett undertook work at Wallington, Northumberland in 1739.[7] Sir Walter may well have known George Bowes at this time. Both became members of Parliament and had coal and lead mining as their main source of wealth. Both used their wealth to develop and improve their estates. Bowes went foxhunting in Northumberland in the 1730s, a pastime also enjoyed by Sir Walter. The men certainly knew each other later when they were both presidents of subscribers to Newcastle Infirmary in 1751[8] and Bowes stayed at Wallington in September 1753. Garrett re-roofed, re-fenestrated and added a central pediment to the south front of Wallington Hall, as well as designing stables and cottages for the estate. His work on the latter led him to produce the first book on farm-house architecture entitled *Designs and Estimates of farmhouses etc. for the County of York, Northumberland, Cumberland, Westmorland and Bishoprick of Durham*, published in 1747.

Bowes' first contact with Daniel Garrett, according to the records, was on 16 November 1740 when the architect was paid ten guineas:

> By Profit and Loss. Paid Geo. Bowes Esqr. wch he gave to Mr. Garret the Architecture £10 10s[9]

There is no mention of the building concerned here, but the amount is the same paid to Etty in 1727 for a plan of the house and gardens at Gibside. It seems likely that the payment was for the building first mentioned in the Cash Accounts on 8 May 1741, when estate labourers were paid for two weeks work leading a keel of limestones to the Gothick Tower. Garrett's new building at Gibside was linked to the making of the octagon pond, and the wish to build a belvedere at a high point from which to view the estate and the surrounding countryside. It is likely that the site was first chosen for its location, rather than the eventual use of the building.

The new building at Gibside was one of the first in the north of England in the Gothick mode. The gothic style had predominated in England well into the 17th century, often in vernacular form. When the new English Palladian style became popular in fashionable circles in the early 18th century, the gothic fell into disuse. However it did not die out, and a new taste for medievalism arose, particularly in follies where a fanciful style of architecture could be indulged.

## *Forerunners of the Gothick Building*

Vanbrugh was one of the first to wish to preserve medieval architecture when he tried to persuade the Duchess of Marlborough to retain the ruins of Woodstock Manor in the grounds of Blenheim Palace. Having sold his estate at Claremont, Surrey, to the 1st Duke of Newcastle in 1714, Vanbrugh designed and built a belvedere tower there in the following year. This gave rise to a fashion for building Gothick towers, which was followed by Lord Bathurst at Cirencester in 1721 and by Lord Islay, afterwards the 3rd Duke of Argyll, at Whitton Park. Here he built a triangular prospect tower 80 feet high, standing at the end of a 370 foot long canal. It is likely that George Bowes saw the tower when he visited his mother-in-law, Mrs. Verney, who lived at Whitton.[10] His visit in September 1737 was four years before his belvedere at Gibside was begun.

James Gibbs designed the Temple of Liberty at Stowe, which was built from 1741-8. This was a complex building, triangular like the tower at Whitton, but with polygonal towers, and small turrets capping two of them, while the third rose to a height of seventy feet. Its Gothick detail referred to the ideal of liberty which it was held the Goths enjoyed, and was part of Lord Cobham's 'political gardening', in which he made the grounds of his house relate to his political views. Work on the new building at Gibside must have started at much the same time as the building of the Temple of Liberty.

## *Follies by Daniel Garrett*

Garrett designed a series of Gothick follies and towers in the north of England, and that at

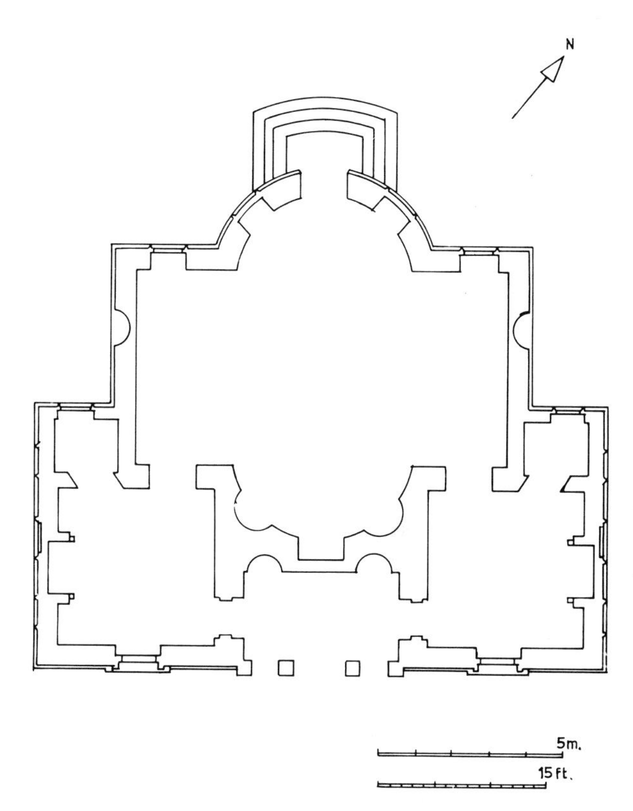


6. Plan of Banqueting House.

Gibside was one of the first. His name is connected with the Temple at Aske, near Richmond in Yorkshire, built for Sir Conyers D'Arcy after his purchase of the estate in 1727. A drawing attributed to Daniel Garrett by Howard Colvin, was found at Inveraray Castle. It was a drawing for the Temple at Aske, as built, and was found together with a drawing for the Temple by William Kent. The drawing by Kent is of a single tower, and the one linked with Garrett is of the Temple as it stands. It seems likely that Garrett either designed the Temple, or acted as clerk of works for its erection. Its date is uncertain. The design for the Temple was ambitious, and consisted of a tower flanked by square turrets rounded at the front. The central doorway had a crocketed frontispiece, and a rounded double string course with a row of blind arches above. The Temple stood on an arcaded podium with an openwork balustrade.

7. The Banqueting House and Column to Liberty.

The Cravensgate Temple at Richmond, Yorkshire was built by Sir Conyers D'Arcy's son-in-law John Yorke. It is easier to date, for it commemorated the battle of Culloden in 1746, and is usually called the Culloden Tower. The tower has also been attributed to Garrett, and it has certain similarities to his work. It is composed as an octagon on a square base, with a taller staircase tower. The band of small blind arches occurs again here, while the tower is surmounted by an openwork balustrade and crockets.

Daniel Garrett's name has been linked with both buildings, either stylistically, or on other evidence. Payments made to Garrett at this time indicate that the new building at Gibside was one of a series of Gothick follies with which he was connected, and may indeed be the first. Bowes was forward-looking in commissioning a Gothick Revival structure, even if the plan was basically a symmetrical Palladian design. The rococo-Gothick decoration successfully masked its simple lines.

### *Bowes' Belvedere*

The new building was referred to in the Cash Accounts as the Gothick Tower for the first eighteen months. For the following year and a half it was referred to as the Gothick Building, and in April 1744 the Tower was again referred to. The accounts however refer to the development of only one building. The new venture was variously described in the estate records as the 'Gothick Building', the 'Tower' or the 'New Building'.

The Gothick Building was fronted by a bay surmounted by three pointed and crocketed pinnacles. Embattled side walls, raised at the corners

8. Interior of Banqueting House, *c.* 1905.

to simulate towers, were enlivened by cross-loops and quatre-foils. The rear entrance was through a triple-bay portico in antis, the cinquefoil heads of which echoed the shape of the windows. To the right of the portico was an ante-room with a closet leading from it. This corresponded to a similar room on the left, which served as a kitchen. Its closet housed a spiral staircase leading to the roof, from which extensive views of the estate could be seen. Both closets had a skew approach, a favourite device of Garrett's, either to preserve symmetry, or to make the entry into a confined space easier.

The Great Room of the Gothick Building could be approached from the two smaller rooms, and was 32 feet long. There were mirrors on the two side walls to give an impression of greater length. A bow on the inner wall contained a chimney-piece with a shell-headed niche on either side. The corresponding outer wall had five cinquefoil headed windows, three of them in the bow. The central opening acted as an additional entrance to the Great Room and was of a kind more usual in greenhouses at that time. When in use the cinquefoil top remained stationary, while the centre was sashed, and below this two curved wooden panels opened inwards to form the entrance. There were hexagonal panes in the sash windows with rounded panes above. William Kent with his inventive flair, had designed a window with hexagonal panes below pointed tracery within an ogee arch, at the Court

9. Gothick Window by Batty Langley.

of the King's Bench, London, in 1739.[11] This may have been known to Garrett and also to Batty Langley, who published a design for a similar sort of window at about this time.

Batty Langley (1696-1751) was the son of a Twickenham gardener and at first followed his father's craft. He later turned to writing about gardening and architecture with his first books aimed at the amateur and the artisan. In 1728 he and his brother Thomas produced *New Principles of Gardening, or the lay-out and planting of Parterres, Groves, Wildernesses, Labyrinths, Parks etc.* in an unsuccessful attempt to secure wealthy patrons. This was on the whole a failure and he and his brother set up an Academy with lessons in architecture and drawing. He was an educator and also a compiler, and the book in which he tried to institute a series of orders for the Gothick, similar to that in classical architecture, was his most original. *Ancient Architecture Restored* appeared in two parts in 1741-2 and in a second edition in 1747, with the more resounding title of *Gothic Architecture, improved by Rules and Proportions*. The Gothick Window which appeared as plate 39 in the second part of the work was published in 1742. It was very similar to the windows designed by Garrett for the Banqueting House. Langley's window had an ogee head flanked by a cusp, while Garrett's window had a cinquefoil top. It would be interesting to know if Garrett or Batty Langley were the originator of this variation on Kent's design.

The walls of the Great Room were stuccoed in a series of shield-like patterns, while the ceiling had an intricate flower motif, which is preserved in Garrett's design in the Strathmore Papers at Durham. Arched niches broke into the ceiling cove, and were repeated in miniature in semi-circular bays and side panels. A similar arcaded cove by Daniel Garrett of 1751-2 still exists in the Hunter's Gallery at Raby Castle. Work on the building began in 1741 and by the following year plasterwork was in progress, indicating that the shell of the building had been completed. The fact that the contents of the building were included in the Gibside Inventory of 1746 shows that Garrett's Banqueting House must have been completed at least five years before he began work on Hunter's Gallery at Raby.

Bowes planned his Belvedere or Tower on the flat land above the Octagon Basin. As the building progressed its purpose became better defined, and on 13 March 1746 Margaret Roy was paid 'for making on Fiers and looking after the Rooms at the Tower and Bath... at one Shilling a wk.' 15s.[12] On 15 May 1746 she was

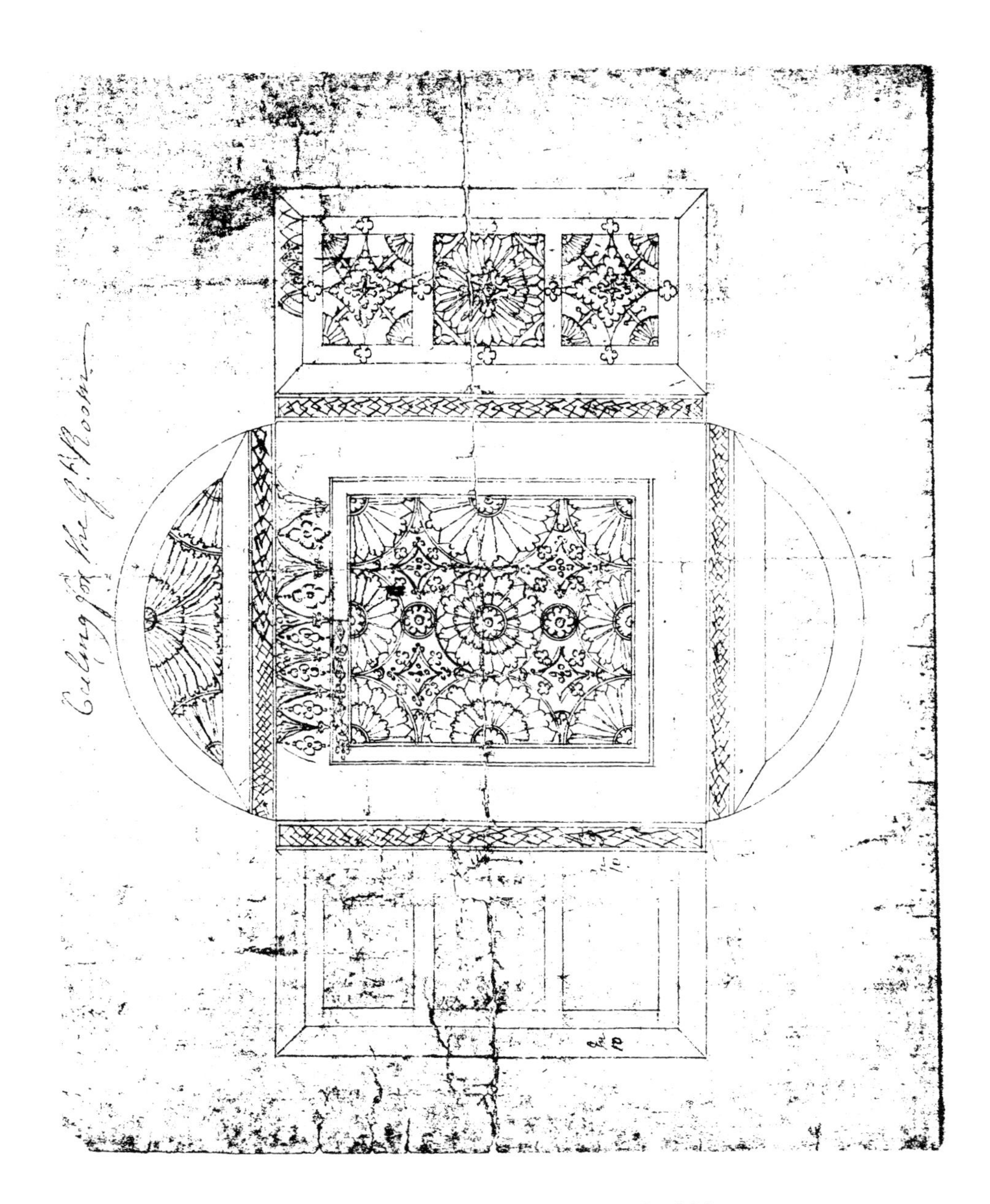

10. Ceiling of Banqueting House, drawing by Daniel Garrett.

11. Plasterwork in Banqueting House.

paid for the same service 'at the Bath and Banquitting house', and the function of the new building was established.

## *The construction of the Banqueting House*

The Gothick Tower had been first mentioned in the Cash Accounts on 8 May 1741, when the estate labourers were paid for leading up a keel of limestones. Other routine tasks were carried out in the next months when stone and other materials were led to the site. Joseph Palliser, the skilled estate carpenter, was roofing the building in October 1741, and by the following July he was 'putting up sealing Joysts and making a Table for the plasterers'. In the following month the Cash Accounts record:

> By Gothic Building. Paid ditto [Joseph Palliser] at the Tower putting up Sealing Joysts, getting wood for Sashes, Horsing Deals and covering the Masons Shade [shed] &c. 13s. 4d[13]

Other work was done by James Watson, a skilled mason, James Walker sharpened tools, and John Nesham did joinerwork. Routine tasks were carried out by estate labourers, who were paid in a body, and must therefore have had a spokesman or foreman to organise their individual payment.

Thomas Dalkin was paid for sash-cord in October 1742, and the five sash windows at the front of the building and the two at the rear, must have been nearing completion. John Carpenter was paid £17 for carving in April 1743 and later that year Joseph Palliser was 'lathing the vestable' [vestabule]. Daniel Garrett must have visited the new building about this time, as the Cash Accounts record on 2 April 1743:

> By Repairs and Improvements. Paid Robt. Dunkin for going to Twisel near Barwick for Mr. Garret six days at two shillings 12s

This leads to speculation as to whether Garrett was involved in building at Twizel where Sir Francis Blake later rebuilt Twizel Castle in the Gothick mode. A further payment was made by Bowes himself to Garrett on 22 October 1743:

> By Repairs and Improvements. Paid George Bowes Esqr. to give Mr. Garret the Archtr. for drawg. plans &c. £21[14]

when plans were specifically mentioned. Drawings for the Gothick Banqueting House formerly existed in the Charter Room at Glamis Castle and may well be the plans referred to here.

The plasterwork was one of the beauties of the Gothick Building. This was undertaken by Philip Daniel, a Swiss *stuccatore* who made his home in England at this time. He was known as Daniel or Danielli. Details of his life are obscure, but his work is recorded in the accounts at Gibside between 1741 and 1768. The other places he is known to have worked are at Duncombe Park, North Yorkshire, Fenham Hall, Newcastle upon Tyne[15] and Nunwick, Northumberland. The decoration of the Hall ceilings at Nunwick bear a distinct resemblance to the plasterwork on the walls of the Ante-Room of the Gothick Building. Here a stylised flower motif in a lozenge is surrounded by a square. He began the stuccowork in the Gothick Building in February 1743. Regular payments were made to him for the rest of that year and his work continued until May 1744. He was usually paid in sums of rather less than £10 per month, with some extra fees for bargain work. His skill can be seen in the restored interiors of both the Great Room and the Ante-Room. The reason why his work is largely unknown is that he spent most of his working life at Gibside.

The estate workers produced elaborately carved shutters and put decorative beading on the door panels of the Ante-Room. The delicacy of the carving contrasted with the more robust plaster niches on the inside wall of the portico. Shell-headed niches relieved the plain outer walls of the Great Room and flanked its fireplace on the inner bow. These niches were a feature of the building, and not necessarily to hold statues, though Bowes did see some 'proper Figures for the Niches on my Banquetting House' when he visited Cheere's sculpture yard in 1751.

While the Banqueting House was being constructed the estate labourers were making the walk below it leading to the Octagon Pond. On the east of the building a fosse was dug to divide its encircling plantations from the fields. Finishing work to the building went on in 1744 when James Walker was paid for 12 cramps for the windows. Work was undertaken 'at the coves and capitals', and in July of that year Joseph Palliser was 'hanging window sheets', while the labourers brought flags from nearby Brasside Moor to pave the vestibule. When Ann Green was paid in November 1744 'for making on Fires at the new building and Bath three weeks' 3s., it was the first sign that the new building was ready for use. It was not until eighteen months later, however, that the purpose of the Gothick Building was made known and the Banqueting House became a functioning part of the Gibside estate. The use of a Banqueting House is still to some extent conjectural. What does seem fairly certain is that the main banquet would be taken in comfort at the mansion and that sweet delicacies and wine would be served after the meal in the Banqueting House. Then the beauties of the estate could be seen from an appropriate viewpoint and hospitality enjoyed.

There was no mention of the Banqueting House in the Inventory of Gibside made in October 1743, shortly after the marriage of George Bowes to Mary Gilbert, his second wife. It does however appear in the Inventory taken in December 1746. It is listed after the rooms in Gibside House, and before the rooms at the Bath. At first the Banqueting House was sparsely furnished. In the Great Room there was:

> a large old Grate, Fire Shovell Poker Tongs and Fender.
> Upon the Chimney Piece Shakespear, Milton and Swift Six Windsor Chairs, one large ditto four Seats

By the time of the next Inventory, over a year after George Bowes' death, more furniture had accumulated in the Banqueting House. By then the Great Room contained:

> twelve Mahogany Chairs, with black leather bottoms, two large fix'd Glasses, Grate shovell poker, Tongs, fender, and an old Grate, some China

It is probable that the last Inventory gives the clearest picture of furniture when the Banqueting House was in use.[16]

## *The Derwent Quays and other works*

Although the greatest amount of building activity during the early 1740s was concentrated on the Banqueting House, other work went on. Trees were planted by the New Coach Way and the Bath Walk turfed in 1740, while the following year the Weirmen were paid for 'filling the Holes below the Bath' and making three weirs in the River Derwent beneath the Bath. Both this bank and the river itself needed constant attention to preserve a well-kept but picturesque effect. Work had begun in 1733 to build retaining walls along the Gibside bank of the River Derwent. These were known as 'keys' in the records and were protective walls five feet high and three feet deep of carefully cut stone blocks of almost ashlar quality. This wall cannot be seen from the land above it and is largely complete round Warren Haugh today. Below the Bath House cliff the embankment or quay has been completely washed away. When this part of the quay was repaired at the end of the eighteenth century the accounts recorded: 'Bath Quay Eastermost part drove away by the River' and nothing of this part of the protective wall now exists. The remains of the quay still run along part of Lady Haugh and then lead inland towards the Old Paper Mill leat. The course of the River Derwent seems to have changed here. The quays cannot have been part of Switzer's plan as he wrote of stone walls in *Ichnographia Rustica:*

> the manner of bounding... round with Walls, is very expensive, and ought to be admitted no where but in the very great Designs of Princes, and for first Rate Designs, because Walling is very expensive...

Bowes must have wished to protect his estate from encroachment by the Derwent. It may have been the fact that there were floods on the River Wear in 1722 and 1727 and these floods may also have occurred on the Derwent, that led Bowes to build the quays.

Some work was done at Gibside House. Thomas Hopes painted the house and mended chimneys, while a new cellar was dug. In June 1743 Philip Daniel broke off his stuccowork at the Banqueting House to undertake some plastering at Gibside House. The following October the labourers were working 'at the New Walk between the pole and the Bason'. This must have been the straight walk which joined the Octagon Basin to the end of the Long or Dove Cote Walk. The latter was subsequently extended westwards to become the Grand Walk. The pole appears to have been placed where these two walks, and a third leading from the old basin, met.

Once the structural work at the Banqueting House was complete, work went on elsewhere. In the summer of 1744 the estate labourers were 'leading Stones and Deals from the Gothick Building to Gibside' and 'leading Timber to the new Wash House'. In July 1744 they were winning and leading stones for the new laundry and wash house, and breaking a door into the Steward's room. A payment was made to Daniel Garrett on 24 December 1745. This was recorded in the Estate Journals immediately after a reference to the new laundry: 'Paid George Bowes Esqr. to give to Mr. Garret ' £10 10s[17] and is likely to have been made in retrospect for its design. The kitchen area at Gibside House seems to have been unsatisfactory, and alterations were made to the offices during the whole of the 18th century. At the same time a new wine cellar was being made, and the brewhouse refurbished.

A new 'Necessary House' two storeys high was also built. It was wainscotted, roofed partly with lead, and was situated in the wood to the west of Gibside House. The upper room of the building had apses on two sides facing each other and vents at the four corners which led to the cess pool below. The lower storey was built into the hillside to make drainage easier. In 1747 a water closet was made. Daniel Garrett had included a water closet in his design for the alterations to Wallington Hall, made in the late 1730s, which was approached from his favourite skew entrance, to give easy access from an ante-room. At Wallington Hall a 'little house' and two privies were also provided at the rear of the house, with an entry from outside the building. A similar arrangement may have been made at Gibside, with the water closet indoors and the Necessary House surrounded by woods.

## *The Jacobite Rebellion of 1745*

George Bowes was occupied with graver matters at this time. The Young Pretender Charles Edward Stuart landed in Scotland on 23 July 1745 and travelled south with his supporters aiming to take London. Bowes took an active part in raising forces against the rebels. Having been a captain in General Wade's regiment in his early youth, Bowes was able to raise, and helped to maintain, a Regiment of Horse under his command for the defence of Durham County. After the Battle of Falkirk, when the rebels were victorious, the Duke of Cumberland travelled north to oppose them. He arrived in Gateshead on 28 January 1746 having journeyed by coach and six from London to Durham:

> but finding that the roads grew worse, his royal highness was pleased to accept of a horse, which was presented to him by George Bowes, esq., M.P. for the county of Durham, upon which he rode into Newcastle[18]

The Duke was victorious over the rebels at the Battle of Culloden on 16 April 1746.

## *The Stables*

Ever since the 1715 rising there had been fears of a second Jacobite attempt. The new rebellion seems to have had little effect on the running of the Gibside estate, and work continued as usual. The approach to Gibside from the highway was still unsatisfactory, and in March 1746 the labourers were 'raising [the] low end of the Coach Road, removing the hill adjoining, levelling and planting'. Buildings at Hollinside, which had been used for extra stabling and as kennels for Bowes' hounds, were altered in 1747, and at the same time the stables at the house itself were proving inadequate. Changes had been made in the stabling in 1726, soon after George Bowes became the owner of Gibside, by 'taking down the Stables at the kitchin *(sic)* end and removing it to the last part of the house and fixing it as it was'. Having the stables so near the house was convenient, but could lead to noxious smells. Like other country house owners at this time Bowes decided to build new stables away from the house, and in the form of the fashionable stable block.

The basic idea was derived from Palladio's villas, which were designed for men who wished to live near the land from which they gained their livelihood. The villas could be relatively simple, and often incorporated stables and other farm buildings either in attached wings or nearby. John Webb (1611-1672) designed a country house with out-houses, barns and stables on the Palladian plan. This was published by William Kent in *The Designs of Inigo Jones* (1727) volume 2, where most of the drawings later proved to be Webb's work. Bowes was a subscriber to the volumes, and may have had Webb's drawing in mind when Garrett designed his new stables.

Stables in Northumberland and Durham up to this time usually consisted of a single range. At Belsay Castle in Northumberland a Jacobean house was built adjoining the 14th century castle. Large and impressive stables were added in the early 18th century. They were built of stone blocks, and plain save for heavy keystones over the doors and windows. The only indication from the outside that the building was for horses was the three coach houses at the north end. The windows looked more suitable for a domestic building than for stabling.

Further south landowners sought to match the Palladian design of their dwelling with stables in the same style. The stable block, often with a pediment over the arch leading to the stable yard, was usually two storeys high and gave accommodation for the horses on the ground floor, with space for feed and living quarters for the grooms above.

Sir Walter Calverley Blackett at Wallington, Northumberland, built some stables in 1735. These were built in two L-shaped ranges some distance to the north of the house with the entry between the two ranges closed by a screen wall and triumphal arch. Walls enclosed the space between the house and the stables forming a large turfed court. The arch proved too narrow for carriages and was replaced by a coach house with a clock tower in the early 1750s. The architect of this handsome building is still not certain. Daniel Garrett had worked at Wallington since before 1740 and it seems likely that he was the designer. It had been attributed to James Paine (1717-1789) in spite of the fact that there is no evidence that Paine visited Wallington before he built the bridge over the River Wansbeck in *c.* 1755. However the drawings for the coach house are not in his hand, but it seems likely that the simple but majestic building was by Garrett and built in 1754.

Stables with a Palladian facade were built at Swinburne Castle, Northumberland, but are unfortunately undated. They were a single two-storey range which on the southern side contained a laundry and drying room, and in the northern part stables. Away from the Castle the building was plain with Palladian detail on the other facades. The central arch and a bay on either side of it projected and were surmounted by a pediment. A relieving arch on the central bay of the wings repeated the central arch, and a thick string course, a block of stone wide, held the composition together.

Bowes now had to decide if he wanted stables which were of a single range, as was usual in Northumberland and Durham, or if he wished to be more ambitious and build a stable block round a courtyard. He chose the latter course but not on the usually accepted Palladian pattern. Daniel Garrett, his architect, had in all probability designed the stables at Temple Newsam on a grand scale for the 7th Viscount Irwin *c.* 1745. These were pedimented on each front and on the south side had a system of openings within three blind arches, which was often used by Garrett. The design for the new stables presented a Palladian facade to those passing along the New Coach Way while the other sides were of plain stone construction.

### *The New Stables*

The first mention of the new stables was in the Cash Accounts for March 1747, when the labourers were 'Leading Stones out of Wheatleys Quarry and dressing ditto for the new Stables'. The building was sited to the south east of Gibside House, on part of the estate known as Horse Close. A payment to Daniel Garrett was recorded in the Cash Accounts on 24 July 1746 'By Repairs. Paid and given Mr. Garret pr. Order' 10 guineas. Again no specific building was mentioned, but the payment is likely to have been for the design of the stables. A larger rectangular version of the plan for the stables still exists at Durham Record Office, but the stables were built on a smaller, square plan. In April 1747 the labourers were pulling down the old stables and work continued until the November of that year, when the foundations of the new

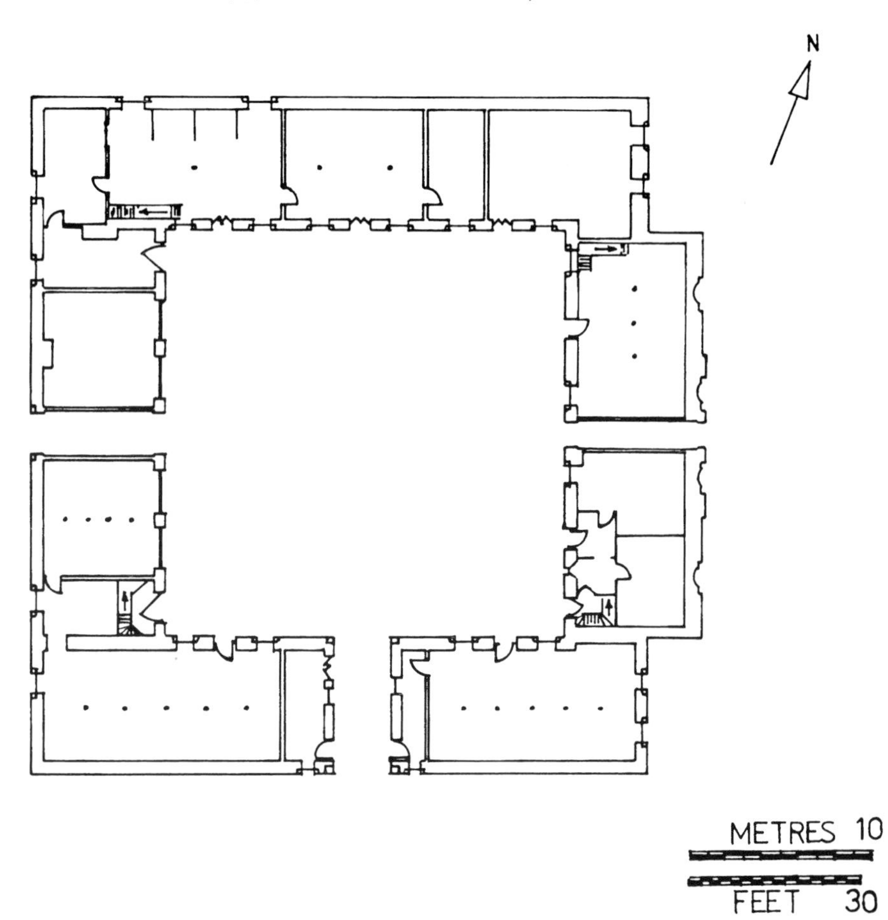


12. Plan of the Stables.

13. The Stables, front view.

stables were dug.[19] By the end of 1749 £1417 17s. 8d. had been spent on the stables, and a further £400 was added by the end of 1751, when the building was virtually complete.

The Palladian east front of the stables had a central doorway on a domestic scale set in a five bay facade. The door was flanked by niches and the centre three bays linked by blind arcades, the same motif as used on the south front of the stables at Temple Newsam. The centre three bays were pedimented and projected slightly. Decorative niches ornamented the lower storeys of the outer bays and a parapet masked most of the roof. Wings on either side of the Palladian centrepiece were set back and had the appearance of pavilions, contrasting with the inner courtyard in the Northumbrian vernacular style. The south side of the quadrangle was the main entrance and had two tall wooden doors. Another arched entrance on the west side meant that a coach could enter through one gateway and exit through the other without reversing. Aubone Surtees supplied 10,000 blue pantiles for the stables in May 1748 and the following July Jonathan Wilkinson was 'Leading the lang Firrs used in planting to hide the East Part of ye Stables'. As this was the Palladian front of the stables it must be supposed that the planting was to frame the building.

Material from the former stables was used to build the new ones. The north wall of the stables was originally windowless and was well built, but the inner wall facing the courtyard was poorly built of re-used stones. In May 1748 the labourers were 'pulling down the old Stables and leading Stones to ye new Stables' and the following April Joseph Palliser was 'putting up Beames under the Granary Joysts and painting Sashes'. In September 1749 Thomas Hopes was turning an Arch in the Lodging Room and making

14. The Stables, South and East fronts.

stalls, while the following February a table was being made for the grooms' room. From this, and the rather ruinous building which still exists, it can be deduced that the lodging was beside and over the southern entrance. There was a granary on the first floor and accommodation for grooms. A great deal of space on the upper floors was used for storing hay and other fodder. This was stored as far as possible over the stalls on floors which did not reach right up to the outer wall. A gap of a foot was left so that hay could easily be sent to the feeding troughs below. There was standing for at least twenty horses, and coach houses on the west side of the courtyard. In his new building Bowes had achieved something that was unusual for the north east, and indeed unusual in that the entrance to the stableyard was not through an entrance in the main facade, but through a plain practical arch to one side. The Palladian front of the building did not need to be used for the horses at all, and made an elegant addition to the buildings near the New Coach Way.

## *Strawberry Castle*

Most of George Bowes buildings were designed to last. One which has disappeared is Strawberry Castle which could perhaps have been designed as a ruin and without the same lasting qualities as his other building ventures. The first reference to Strawberry Castle was made in August 1746 when Philip Daniel, the Swiss plasterworker, was paid for 'plastering the Castle in the wood'.[20] In December 1747 the estate labourers were making a road to the Castle and in October 1748 Thomas

Gray, an estate worker, was paid 'for Carving the Cornish [cornice] and Pedestall in Strawbery Castle', so that the building must have had some architectural elements. Unfortunately the site of this building is not known. Strawberry Castle existed for at least 30 years, for in June 1778 the Cash Accounts record 'leading Grass to the Walks, Gravel to Strawberrie Castle'.

Bowes had now built the Banqueting House in the Gothick mode and perhaps Strawberry Castle in the same manner, but it was not he but Sir Hugh Smithson who made the style fashionable in the north east. When Lady Smithson inherited the Percy Estate in Northumberland she and her husband decided to make Alnwick Castle their summer residence. The newly created Earl and Countess of Northumberland preferred Alnwick to the castle at Warkworth as it was more easily accessible. The Countess was enthusiastic about the Gothick style, which was not to her husband's taste, but seemed ideal for the site. She and her husband began rebuilding the Castle about 1752, at first with the help of Daniel Garrett, and on his death in 1753 James Paine designed a grand staircase and some rooms in the keep. He was superseded by Robert Adam (1728-1792) who was working there by 1768. He made a suite of rooms in the Gothick style with elegant plasterwork, which unfortunately no longer exists. He also designed buildings in the grounds such as the observatory-teahouse at Ratcheugh Crag and the tower at Brizlee of 1777, based on designs of the ubiquitous Batty Langley. The Earl was created Duke of Northumberland in 1766, when he virtually retired from the court in exchange for the dukedom. He was the richest man in the county, with great political power, and wielded much influence. It was his example, not that of George Bowes, that led to a surge of buildings in north east England with embattled walls, cross-loops and quatre-foil decoration. George Bowes' Banqueting House did not have such an influence, but he was one of the first, if not the first, in the north to adopt the Gothick Revival style.

Bowes had now completed improvements near the house, and made alterations to the house itself. The Bath House and river walks were in use, and the basic plan for walks in the vicinity of the house carried out. The Octagon Basin and the Banqueting House were complete, and in addition the building of the new stables gave added dignity to the approach to Gibside House. Bowes now wished to make a vista to the south of the house, and to undertake even more ambitious plans.

CHAPTER

# 5

# *New Beauties*

## *Bowes' Prestige*

Bowes had by 1747 reached a position of standing in the county. He had been a member of Parliament for the County of Durham for twenty years, he had been mayor of Durham on two occasions and twice mayor of Hartlepool. He had been chairman of the Grand Jury many times and was an able and active magistrate. His public spirit and patriotism had been proved by his raising and maintaining troops against the Jacobites in the rebellion of 1745. His threats to William Cotesworth, and the duel with one of the Claverings, were regarded as youthful lapses. He had been unsuccessful in his efforts to become a freeman of Newcastle upon Tyne, where a strong Tory faction held sway, and his request had been finally refused in 1741. In Durham County, however, although he had his enemies, he was respected and esteemed.

He married for a second time in June 1743. His bride was Mary Gilbert of St. Pauls Walden Bury, Hertfordshire. She was the heiress of her father, Edward Gilbert. Between 1720 and 1725 Gilbert laid out the gardens at the Bury with hedge-lined grassy walks enclosing plantations of trees, the vistas being terminated mainly by statues. These gardens had been designed before George Bowes began to plan his own estate, but his father-in-law's use of rides through trees must have appealed to him, as he used much the same idea at Gibside from 1729 onwards. Bowes paid his father-in-law the compliment of naming Mr. Gilbert's walk after him. Bowes' careful stewardship of his estate at Gibside was matched by his care for the Bowes' ancestral seat at Streatlam Castle in the south of County Durham. The castle had been largely rebuilt by William Blakiston Bowes in 1721 shortly before he died. George Bowes kept up the estate, and visited it occasionally, though he did not live there. A third property, Wemmergill Hall in Lunedale, was also kept in repair, and Bowes hoped that the smelt mill on the moors nearby would prove profitable.

As well as these properties, and many others which Bowes inherited or bought to further his coal interests, he rented two properties which he used as staging posts on visits to London. One of these was Newstead Abbey, Nottinghamshire, which Bowes rented for £200 a year from 1738-46. The house had belonged to the Byron family since the Reformation, and there was a distant connection been the Bowes and Byron families. The remains of the former Priory Church stood next to the house and was a romantic reminder of past times. The 4th Lord Byron was the first to improve the grounds, and in 1695 added a canal, a pond and formal garden in the style of Le Nôtre (1613-1700), the French royal landscape architect. The house was in a coal-mining area, as was the other house Bowes rented shortly afterwards, Ledston Hall in Yorkshire. The grounds of the hall had been altered by their owner, Lady Betty Hastings, who employed Charles Bridgeman to improve the grounds in 1731. On Lady Betty's death the estate passed to her half-brother, the 9th Earl of Huntingdon, and as he had no wish to live there he let it to George Bowes. The formal element in the grounds must have suited Bowes as the lease continued from 1741 to his death in 1760.

## *The Grand Walk*

At Gibside Bowes now turned his attention to the south west part of the estate. He wished to carry out one of Switzer's suggestions, to make a grand avenue. Although this had become an old-fashioned feature since Kent banished the straight line, it suited George Bowes because of its grandeur, and the broad grassy avenue gave him an opportunity to race his bloodstock. It was situated on one of the few relatively flat parts of the estate once it rose from the water meadows, with differences in level to either side of it being retained by walls and ditches. Work on the Grand Walk began in October 1746 and by the following August the Cash Accounts record 'By Grand Walk Paid ditto [Thomas Hopes] pulling down the Dove Coat and old Barn'.[1] The removal of these two buildings made the continu-

15. The Grand Walk.

ation of the Dove Cote Walk, now named the Grand Walk, possible. Work levelling and banking proceeded, and in November 1747 tree planting began:

> By The Grand Walk. Paid John Hague to give the Gardr. at Lumley on bringing Elms from thence to plant in ditto walk [£] 2.2.0 and paid ditto to give the people at the Gate 2s 6d in all.[2]

Work went on until the following April bringing further trees from Lumley and planting them in the avenue. By June the Grand Walk was being railed off to preserve the newly planted trees, and in July a leather pipe was bought for the watering cart to keep them moist. Work on the Grand Walk continued until 1749. In a letter written to his sister in 1760 Bishop Pococke recalled an earlier visit to Gibside in 1747 when George Bowes:

> carryd me from Durham to his house here and showing me, or taking care that I should see, every thing curious in the country. He was then making the fine green terrace which is very broad, and about a measured mile long, just before the house; we came through a lawn on the river with single trees in it, and turned up by the wood (by the road which leads to the house) in which there are winding walks on the side of the hill, which lead to a summer-house at this end.[3]

From Bishop Pococke's description it appears that he and his host approached Gibside from the direction of Friarside to the south west, which is the present-day entrance. At that time it was a path or bridle way, and perhaps Bowes wished to show his guest the Grand Walk before he saw the rest of the estate.

## *The Ice House*

The second Mrs. Bowes is rather an enigmatic figure, but it was perhaps by her wish that the Ice House was built. In July 1747 William Cranston was sent from Ravensworth Castle with some ice. The following February an entry in Mrs. Bowes Cash Accounts, under House Expence, ran 'Paid & given Lord Ravensworth's Gardener for Fruit and Ice from Ravensworth' 10s 6d. A letter from Richard Stephenson, Bowes' agent at Gibside, followed some months later:

> Mr. Jones. Gardener at
> Ravensworth Castle.
> Gibside 15th Sept. 1748. Thursday.
> My Master desires you'll send by the bearer two Pails of Ice. And it would be a particular favour if you could bring a Basket of Fruit tomorrow about Ten o'Clock.
> I am Sir, Yor. [Humble ?] Servt.
> R. Stephenson.[4]

If this were a stratagem to hasten the building of an ice house it proved successful. In October 1748 Thomas Hopes was paid for building up an arch at the Ice House, and John Maugham for sawing joists. Joseph Palliser was 'Joysting, Roofing and making Centers for the Ice House' and in November Thomas Hopes was building the Ice House porch. The porch embraced a short passage five feet long between two doors, and by December 1749 Thomas Hopes was 'making a threshold for the Ice House'. The building was thatched, partly with ling, for insulation and corfe rods were used for stands. The bottom part of the Ice House was of an inverted bee-hive construction made of rosy red brick, 18 feet deep and approximately 25 feet across. The top of the structure was a brick groin vault of concentric rings with cross arches on either side of the entrance. With such a building situated above the stream leading to the Bath House bridge, Bowes never again had to ask Ravensworth Castle for ice or fresh fruit.

## *The Gibside Household*

Mrs. Bowes also had an influence on the rooms at Gibside House. In the 1746 Inventory the Missasippy Room was listed, but the gaming table had been removed and the 'Missasippy Table carry'd to Sotts Hall'.[5] The Gaming Room seems to have become the Prayer Room by the 1761 Inventory, though the Sotts Hall still remains. The change must have been made some time before as there were 'Repairs to Prayer Room hangings' in December 1750. Mrs. Bowes was also a keen reader of books and bought a great number. She did not buy Daniel Garrett's *Designs and Estimates for Farm Houses* (1747) but the following May her Cash Accounts recorded: 'By Accot. of Books. Paid Mr Garret for 6 of his Plans for building Farm houses' £3 13s 6d.[6]

In the grounds at Gibside as the programme of new works progressed, the older buildings were well maintained. The Bath House, and the cliff below it, needed constant attention, and the fosse encircling the eastern limits of the Banqueting House plantation needed care. Other maintenance, such as mowing and rolling large areas of grass, and clipping hedges, were regularly carried out. Bowes had an eye for detail, and was fond of statuary. In 1735 statues were led from Dunston, on the south bank of the Tyne, and at that time were no doubt intended for the Bath House. A realistic lead statue of a gunner was painted and set up near the Derwent, and in 1751 Bowes was considering buying from Cheere's Figure Shop in London 'Prior & Congreve proper Needs for my Bath' at £15 each. In the 1761 Inventory there were busts of Pope and Dean Swift in the 'far dining room' at Gibside House, and 'six figures upon the Chimney piece' in the Banqueting House.

It is not certain when Bowes met the influential Sir Hugh Smithson. It may have been through Sir Thomas Robinson, whose house at Rokeby was near Sir Hugh's home at Stanwick Hall. On 27 April 1746 the Gibside Journals record 'Paid Sr. Hugh Smithson the first payment of a Subscription to Statues' £1, but there is no record of a subsequent payment. After Smithson had been created Earl of Northumberland in 1750 the friendship between the two men gradually waned.

Mrs. Bowes' Cash Accounts of 18 January 1749 record ten pictures bought at an auction in Pall Mall. They are given under the heading 'Household goods', and include two landscapes, three pieces with figures by Rubens and a history piece by Paolo Veronese. The new pictures would give variety to the collection at Gibside, which up to that time had consisted of family portraits and engravings.

Into this discerning and prosperous household Mary Eleanor Bowes was born on 24 February 1749. She was named Mary after George Bowes' second wife, and Eleanor after his first. He received a letter of congratulation from Captain William Fitzthomas dated 2 March:

> What tho' it be'nt a Boy, the same Material will produce one, be industrious & apply yourself closely to the Business, & I warrent your success.

He added 'at least your Blood, if not your Name will be transmitted to Posterity'. He also mentioned a relative of his, in some way connected with the Bowes, now seven years old, who might be prevailed on to take the name of Bowes and make a match of it.[7]

To pass the time while Mrs. Bowes 'lay in for the Month' at her daughter's birth she bought a six volume edition of the *History of Tom Jones* and later a silver brooch for the child. Under contingency expenses Mrs. Bowes' Cash Accounts recorded 'Paid Mr. Bowes for the Childs Corral he bought' £2 2s. In June the bellringers of Gateshead were paid a guinea 'for Ringing on the News of Miss Bowes' Birth'.

The child's birth meant a new will, which was made at Gibside on 7 February 1750, nearly a year after the birth of his daughter.[8] By the terms of the will, if Bowes had no son, his property was left in trust for his daughter Mary Eleanor. There were six trustees, four from Bowes' family, Thomas Rudd of Durham City and Sir Hugh Smithson. Later the trusteeship was confined to members of the family by a codicil. Bowes ensured that if he died without male issue, any suitor for his daughter, Mary Eleanor, would have to assume the name of Bowes. He also willed, that should the direct line fail any successor would have to take the name of Bowes.

Having established that the family collieries should continue to be run as he directed, he considered the guardianship of his daughter, and made generous provision for her care and education until she became twenty-one.

He then turned to a project very dear to his heart, and directed that the trustees should use the yearly profit from his collieries to:

> lay out the Sum of Two Thousand Pounds in Building a Chappel at the West end of the Great Walk at Gibside which Sum shall be so laid out within the space of six years after my death...

Having fixed the salary of the Minister, Bowes continued 'And my further will is that a good Vault be made in the said Chappell where I desire I may be buried'. Thus his projected chapel was to become his mausoleum.

The Grand Walk, or as Bowes referred to it in his will the 'Great Walk' at Gibside was completed in the same year as his will. Bowes had created a broad terrace over 60 feet wide, which formed a viewpoint from which to see the southern part of the estate. It did not, at this stage, lead anywhere. At the eastern end was a valley and Snipes Dene Wood, and at the other it fell ignominously into Leap Mill Burn. However by prolonging the line of the avenue it would reach an eminence in Snipes Dene Wood. It was here that George Bowes decided to raise a monumental column.

## *The Column*

George Bowes had already achieved Addison's Image of Liberty by taking advantage of the natural features of the steeply sloping land at Gibside, ridged with streams falling into the Derwent. The idea that the column should bear the figure of Liberty was not decided at the outset. In George Bowes' Memorandum Book for 1751, now at Glamis, there is mention of purchases to be made of 'Chair, The Figure Shop'. The Cheere brothers, Henry and John were sculptors, and at first in partnership. John Cheere (1709-1787) then took over John Nost's sculpture yard at the Haymarket while his brother worked at his yard in Hyde Park Corner. Both had aristocratic clients. Henry Cheere

16. The Column to Liberty.

(1703-1781) made funerary monuments and chimney-pieces while his brother specialized in figures for a landscape setting. It is likely that it was John Cheere's yard that Bowes visited to find a figure for his column. Bowes noted of his visit to Cheere:

> He recommends for my Column Jupiter, Diana or Aurora, says they cant be carried not raised if above 12 foot high. Vid. the height of the Figures at St. Pauls. Ditto the Figure on Bloomsbury Church. Q what Figures on Ld. Cobhams or the Duke of Marlboroughs Columns. Prior & Congreve proper Needs for my Bath...Venus & Mercury leaning on a Tyhers Skin Plaister proper Figures for the Niches on my Banquetting House, Charges 7 £ each. Therewith a good Hera of the same dimensions.[9]

Cheere's sculpture yard did not however provide a figure for the column, and it was carved by Christopher Richardson (1709-1781) of Doncaster.

Capability Brown (1716-1783) was born at Kirkharle in Northumberland and at first worked for Sir William Loraine at the nearby Hall. He moved to Stowe in 1741 remaining there for ten years. He had designed a column to his late master, Lord Cobham in 1747, and was consulted about the column at Gibside. In answer to a letter from Bowes' agent Richard Stephenson, Brown gave details about the height and dimensions of Lord Cobham's column. He wrote from Stowe in October 1750:

> The Pillar with its Capitel and Bace are of The Tuscan Proportion, but of defert: Members, which I composed, to make it more monumental, and to answer The Octagonal forme of the Pillar.

Brown offered to help in the construction of the Gibside column:

> ...if you would pleas to send me a rough Sketch of it, with the Weight of a Cubick Foot of The Stone I will put you in the Way that you will be Sure to have your Building Stand.

He added that the scaffolding was of the greatest importance after the foundations. His letter ended:

> If I can be the least useful to you I beg you may Command me because I Should have a double pleasure in it your Situation being my Native County.[10]

His offer was not taken up, but Bowes made sure that his column was taller and with a larger statue than that at Stowe.

Although there is no documentary evidence of the architect for Bowes' column, it is likely to have been Daniel Garrett. He appears to have built a similar column, on a much smaller scale, for Sir Hugh Smithson at Stanwick Hall. The column was dedicated to the Peace of Aix-la-Chapelle in 1748, and bore a statue of Apollo Belvedere. It would have given Garrett suitable experience for the building of a column three times its size. Bowes planned that his column would overtop all others in Great Britain, save for Wren's Monument commemorating the

Great Fire of London (1671-7), which was 202 feet high. When built Bowes' column was 132 feet 10 inches high, with the added height of the figure and its base to surmount it, making a total height of just over 146 feet. On Garrett's death in 1753 supervision of the finishing of the column was taken over by James Paine.

James Paine (1717-1789) trained probably in London at St. Martin's Lane Academy. Here he gained a knowledge of Rococo design from Hubert Gravelot (1699-1773) the engraver, and came into contact with the Palladian architect Isaac Ware (*c.*1717-1766). His first employment was at Nostell Priory, Yorkshire, where he acted as clerk of works, a post that may have been due to the influence of Lord Burlington. Work at Nostell lasted seven years until 1744, when he obtained a commission to design Heath House a few miles away. In 1745 Paine was appointed Clerk of Works at the Queen's House, Greenwich, and was promoted in the following year. From 1747 he designed a number of houses in and around Doncaster, and in 1753, on the death of Daniel Garrett, appears to have taken over his practice and doubled the number of his commissions. This corresponds to what took place with other Garrett commissions where Paine took over his work and completed it. There were four entries for James Paine's work on the column in Mrs. Bowes' Cash Accounts:

> 20 Oct. 1753 By The Column expence. Pd. and given Mr. Payne for his advice relating the column 2 " 2 " –
>
> 20 Aug. 1754 By Column Expence. Pd. Mr. Bowes he gave Mr. Paine the Architect 10 "10 " –
>
> 5 Sept 1754 By Column expence. Paid Mr. Bowes he gave Mr. Paine the Architect 5 " 5 " –
>
> 13 July 1756 By the Column expence. Paid Mr. Paine the Architect 10 "10 " –

## *The Building of the Column*

The first mention of the column in the Gibside Estate Journals is on the 24 and 29 September 1750, before the letter was received from Capability Brown. The Journal records 'By the Column Building £3 " 18 " 5' and refers to boring for foundations, and winning stones at Wheatleys Quarry.[11] Wheatleys Quarry was at Crook Gate, a mile and a half south of the hill in Snipes Dene Wood. From the quarry the stone would be led north to Cut Thorn Farm, and then by the straightest road possible across the valley to the site of the column. By September 1751 they were covering in the foundations, and in the summer of 1752 scaffolding was being erected. In October and November 1753 the scaffolding was taken down. Daniel Garrett's death must have caused uncertainty about completion of the column and at this point James Paine was called in, the scaffolding re-erected and the building resumed.

Bowes was not yet sure of the height of the figure he wished to place on the column, or what it would represent. His visit to John Cheere's figure shop in 1751 had proved inconclusive, and in 1756 he investigated the height of the figures on the pediment of St. Pauls Cathedral and of a figure at St. George, Bloomsbury, which he had noted after his visit to Cheere's yard. He found that the height of the figures on the pediment of St. Paul's were 12 feet, while the painted figures in the dome were 14 feet. He also visited Hawksmoor's St. George, Bloomsbury and found that the statue of George I, rather incongrously perched on its steeple, was 11 feet high.[12]

Apart from the height of the figure, he was also concerned about the size of stone produced by his quarry, which would only yield blocks up to three feet square. This worried him also on account of the size of the columns needed for his proposed chapel. In an entry in his memorandum book headed 'The Figure for the Column' he wrote:

> The Stone in my Quarry wont rise above 3 feet & seems in that thickness & whether that Thickness will answer for the Columns on the intended Chapl.

This entry in his memorandum book was made 24 June 1756, when the height of the column was

17. Profile of the Statue of Liberty.

123 feet, and he considered that the figure 'ought to be above 12ft 6 in'. Bowes' meticulous calculations of the sizing of the stones for the figure show that it was to be made of three stones, the two lower being 4 feet high, and the one for the head and shoulders 4ft. 6 in. He mentioned that there should be a model of the figure and 'I agreed Richardson of Doncaster to give him Forty pounds to carve the Figure'. Richardson sculpted the statue of six blocks of stone. The base and legs to below the knee were made of two blocks, joined vertically, with four courses of stone for the rest of the work. The figure including the base, which was an integral part of the work, measured 13 feet 2 1/2 inches. The carving was fine and delicate with great attention to detail. The previous April Corney Stephenson had paid Mr. Water 5s. 'for an effigy of Liberty', which must have proved unsatisfactory as Bowes commissioned Christopher Richardson.

Richardson often worked in association with Paine, who wrote to Bowes from Chatsworth:

Geo. Bowes Esqr.

Sir,

I am favoured with your orders fr. Mr Stephenson, and for Answer, think the Cap & Staff rising Abo the head of the figure make a better Groop and particularizes the caracter preferable to the height in the model. I think the proportion of the Cap & Staff in this drawing is not to be mended. The Joints also I think, do very well and can see no Objection to any one part, nor to the Whole. I wish I could pay my respects to you this Summer at Gibside, but thats not in my power, as my business hasten me back to London.

I am Sir with Great<br>Respect<br>Your most Hoble servant<br>Jas. Paine

Chatsworth July 27th 1757[13]

In February and March 1757 Thomas Hopes and other workmen were winning stones for the figure to represent Liberty, and Joseph Palliser made a shed to protect the sculptor when he completed work on the figure in situ on the column. On 30 November Henry Reed was given £8 14s. 'For a Copper Staff and Cap for the Figure'. The Gibside Journals made explicit reference to the emblems of Liberty. Thomas Charlton was paid £5 15s 6d. 'for 66 books of Leaf Gold for Gilding the Figure'. The column was nearing completion. Flags and a drainage channel had still to be laid round the base of the column, the surrounding area grassed, a suitable approach made, and the work would be complete.

The final amount for building the column was £1,601 18s 9¾d. and was reached at the end of December 1759. From the accounts Joseph Palliser was responsible for carpentry work, James and John Walker for smith's work, Thomas

Hopes for winning stones, and William Hall and his son for winning and dressing stone. Other workmen were called in to act as labourers, or for specialised craft work.

The column was truly monumental. There was a sturdy pedestal, and rising above it 51 courses of greyish buff stone forming an elegant Roman Doric column. On the abacus was a drum with a tall capstan-shaped support for the statue of Liberty. She was dressed in classical drapery with her hair drawn into a knot at the back of her head. Her slim ankles were supported at the back by a tree trunk in the manner of marble copies of Greek bronzes. Her left hand held the folds of her skirt, and her right the staff of Maintenance and cap of Liberty, which also feature in the coronation of a British monarch. She looked over the valley to the house below her.[14]

Exuberant nationalism appeared in the middle of the eighteenth century. As well as the Jacobite uprising 1745 saw the birth of 'Rule Britannia', which was published anonymously in *The Gentleman's Magazine* for that year, and is reputed to be written by Dr. John Bull. 'God Save the King', with words by James Thomson, was introduced during the Stuart rebellion and became the first national anthem in the world. Britannia was closely associated with Liberty, both graphically and as a concept. James Thomson in his poem 'Liberty' referred to the staff of Maintenance and cap of Liberty and the statue may well have been based on a description such as that in Thomson's poem.

The concept of freedom had been celebrated in the Gothic Temple at Stowe by James Gibbs dedicated 'To the Liberty of our Ancestors' (1744), while at Wentworth Woodhouse the Hoober Stand by Henry Flitcroft (1697-1769) was built in 1748. It was dedicated to George II 'Preserver of our Religion, Laws and Libertys'. In his Column to Liberty George Bowes was instrumental in creating a monument which was unusual even for the time. George Clarke, author of a history of the garden buildings at Stowe, which appeared in *The Stoic,* the magazine of Stowe School, wrote:

> The Gibside statue is a curious piece, as curious as any at Stowe, but the idea of course belongs to the same political group, or, at any rate, to the same philosophical circle.

Nowhere in the Gibside records was the statue referred to as of 'British Liberty' and this description must have grown up as part of the patriotic feeling of the time. Thirty years later William Hutchinson referred to 'the elegant gilt statue of British Liberty' in his *History and Antiquities of the County Palatine of Durham* (1787).

George Bowes planned the column as a monument in landscape, to beautify his grounds. It was an expression of his wealth, standing and influence. By the choice of statue to surmount it, made when the column itself was nearly finished, he transformed it into a symbol of Whig supremacy.

## *The Hollow Walk and West Wood Way*

The denes which crossed the Gibside Estate meant that some excavation and infilling had to be carried out to make the nineteen Gibside Walks possible. The Hollow Walk, which was a continuation of the Grand Walk towards the Column to Liberty, crossed a stream from near the Stables and the overflow from the Octagon Pond. These were culverted and the valley partly filled in to make an easy path, which met the rides from the Old Basin and the Octagon Pond. The walk was retained by walling where the land fell steeply away, with buttresses to support the wall above the culverts.

The West Wood Way was begun in 1749 before the building of the column began. This started from a ride near the Hall Field, which it skirted until the West Wood was reached. A small ha-ha protected the wood from straying cattle. It then followed the line of Leap Mill Burn to join the path to Friarside. The construction took two years, and was perhaps the last of the circuits planned by Switzer.

## *The Park and Alterations to Gibside House*

Reinhold Angerstein, the director of a Swedish Steelworks, visited the Crowley ironworks in the lower Derwent valley, and wrote of Gibside in 1754:

> a splended park with its green pathways, the beautiful garden and the magnificent buildings, which according to English custom are spread about the park. They consist of a summer-house located on a hillock, and built in the gothic style, lovely and pleasant, a pool according to the Greek taste, adorned with a number of statues, and a column, now being erected, which is going to be dedicated to Minerva...
>
> When one walks in the avenues along the river, one may unexpectedly catch sight of a gunner taking aim. He looks very natural, but is cast of lead and painted.[15]

Bowes could now enjoy his estate and show it off to his friends and neighbours. Another coal-owner, Edward Montagu of Denton Hall, wrote to his wife Elizabeth:

> I dined this day sennight at Gibside; it was one of the finest summer days I ever saw.... All the gentlemen are planting and adorning their Seats, but nothing comes up to the grandeur and magnificence of what Mr. Bowes has done, and is adoing, I mean without doors, for his house is an indifferent one. It stands in the midst of a great wood of about 400 acres, through which there are a great many noble walks and rides inter-spers'd with fine lawns, with a rough river running thro' it, on each side of which are very high rocks, which gives it a very romantick look. Mr. Bowes is at present upon a work of great magnificence, which is the erecting a column of above 140 feet high... I ought not to omit telling you that he has already erected upon a rising ground a gothick building which he calls a Banquetting room, in which the night before there was a concert of Musick, at which Jordain and an Italian woman performed...[16]

A few years later on his visit to Gibside in 1760, Bishop Pococke described the estate to his sister:

> We then rid out a mile through the woods having a view of the pillar in some places... The whole ride through these plantations is about two measured miles.[17]

The Bishop also referred to Gibside House:

> There was an old house, of the style of building used in the time of King James I. to which they have made addition in the same line and a return.

In April 1753 Thomas Hopes was paid for 'Walling up six Windows in the Front of the Hall', and a bill in the accounts for 1754 mentioned 'Drawing Plans of the new rooms' on 1 December 1753 and 3 February 1754. In January 1754 Thomas Hopes plastered the new bed chamber and cellar and later also worked on the kitchen stair. During May the new bedchamber was wainscotted and a marble chimney put in place. The following August a door was broken into the new drawing room, windows put into the room above, and the drawing room windows enlarged.[18] Finishing touches were also made to the new study. By 1755 plastering was in progress, and in June Joseph Palliser was 'putting in the Drawing Room Sashes'. The new additions to the house seemed to be complete.

Bowes was still competing for his seat as one of the two candidates for Durham County whenever a parliamentary election was announced. In the election called in April 1754 the other candidate to run with Bowes was Henry Vane, Lord Barnard. The joint expenses came to over £800 and included stabling bills and servants' drinking. On April 26th a ball to celebrate the victory was held and a bill from Cath Proud for the shared expenses listed:

| | £ | s | d |
|---|---|---|---|
| Tea & Chocolate | | | |
| Mackeroons & Biskeets | 6 | 3 | 4 |
| Cards 6 packs | 0 | 6 | 6 |
| | 6 | 9 | 10 |
| ye Room | 3 | 3 | 0 |
| a Moiety 4.16 | | | |
| | 9 | 12 | 10 |

At Gibside alterations to the mansion were continuing and, according to the copy of James Stephenson's map of the estate made in 1767, the new wing extended to the south of the house for a considerable distance. Attached to it were more kitchen offices, joined to the new wing, but not as yet forming a courtyard. Further alterations were carried out by James Paine in 1760. He wrote to Bowes:

> Immediately after I recd. yr. Directions at

> Gibside, I gave orders for making yor. Four Glass Frames for yor. Drawing Room at Gibside, and also the Paper ornament for the Cove.[19]

At the same time various rooms in Gibside House were repainted, a new chimney-piece carved, and Philip Daniel undertook some stuccowork.

In a letter dated 3 October 1758 Bowes' health seemed precarious:

> I thank God I am so much better with a little Rest I had last night, & the Night before, that I flatter myself I shall have the pleasure of seeing my friends in the North before the close of Holy days & my Physician thinks such a Journey will contribute greatly to my perfect Recovery.[20]

It was perhaps thoughts of mortality which made him return to a project he had first considered more than twenty years before – to build a chapel.

CHAPTER
# 6
# *The Chapel*

When Bowes had completed the Grand Walk at Gibside in 1749 he had to decide how the avenue could best be terminated. If the proposed chapel had been sited at the east end of the Grand Walk it would have been near the house, and conveniently situated for its users, but it would have meant that the family and their guests would have had little reason to visit the south western part of the estate. Its location at the west end of the avenue meant that it was the objective of another of the Gibside Walks, and could also be reached from the West Wood Way. Bowes had chosen a monumental column to terminate the eastern end of the Grand Walk, providing a conspicuous landmark visible not only to those on his estate, but to others in the Derwent valley. A chapel would provide an imposing contrast to his Column to Liberty.

## *Early design for a Chapel at Gibside*

Bowes had first thought of building a chapel at Gibside in the 1730s. He had been deeply affected by the death of his first wife at the early age of fourteen, after only two and a half months of marriage. He wrote to her mother the Honourable Mrs. Verney: 'My Dear is dead & after such a loss nothing can happen worthy of my regard'[1] Bowes planned to go abroad, but his mother-in-law thought he should marry again. Four years later he wrote from Gibside to the Honourable John St. John congratulating him on his happiness:

> all such agreeable prospects are vanished from my Breast, and there remains nothing but blank despair. The most nauseous draught of Life that imbitters all other enjoyments.[2]

From his letters, both to Mrs. Verney and others, Bowes seemed at first inconsolable. He immersed himself in coal trade matters, and turned to the planning of Gibside for relaxation. He wrote of his progress to Mrs. Verney, who replied on 25 September 1736:

> I approve of all your improvements, but if you intend to build a Chappell will not an inscription there be properer for my Relation.[3]

The first evidence for such a building is a plan dated 1737,[4] the year following Mrs. Verney's letter to her son-in-law about the chapel. The plan was of a circular building, with engaged columns on either side of a niche in the four segments of the interior. The plan resembled the Villa Rotonda with its projecting porticos, and was a symmetrical Palladian design. There is no indication of the architect. The two most likely people to have been concerned were Sir Thomas Robinson, George Bowes' old friend, or Robinson's protégé Daniel Garrett. There are similarities between the plan and that of Hawksmoor's Mausoleum at Castle Howard. Sir Thomas would have known the plan well, as he had tried to make Hawksmoor change its design on more than one occasion. After Hawksmoor's death in 1736, control for completing the setting of the Mausoleum passed to Sir Thomas, who gave Daniel Garrett the task of building its steps and court. Both men were well acquainted with the Castle Howard Mausoleum, but whether the amateur architect or his protégé were concerned in the early plan for a chapel at Gibside can not be established.

The plan for a chapel was set aside, and Bowes became engrossed in other projects for his estate. His will of 1750 reaffirmed his intention to build a chapel, which was to contain his mausoleum, but delayed the building until after his death. He had been ill in 1758 and again at the beginning of 1760, when Lord Strathmore wrote from Lisbon on 3 May 1760 saying that he had a good report of George Bowes' health. By 9 June there was a deterioration and Bowes had trouble with his lungs, spitting phlegm and blood.[5] Bowes must have decided that now there could be no delay, and he wished to be involved in the building of his chapel.

Map 4 Original map of Gibside, by James Stephenson, 1767, detail.

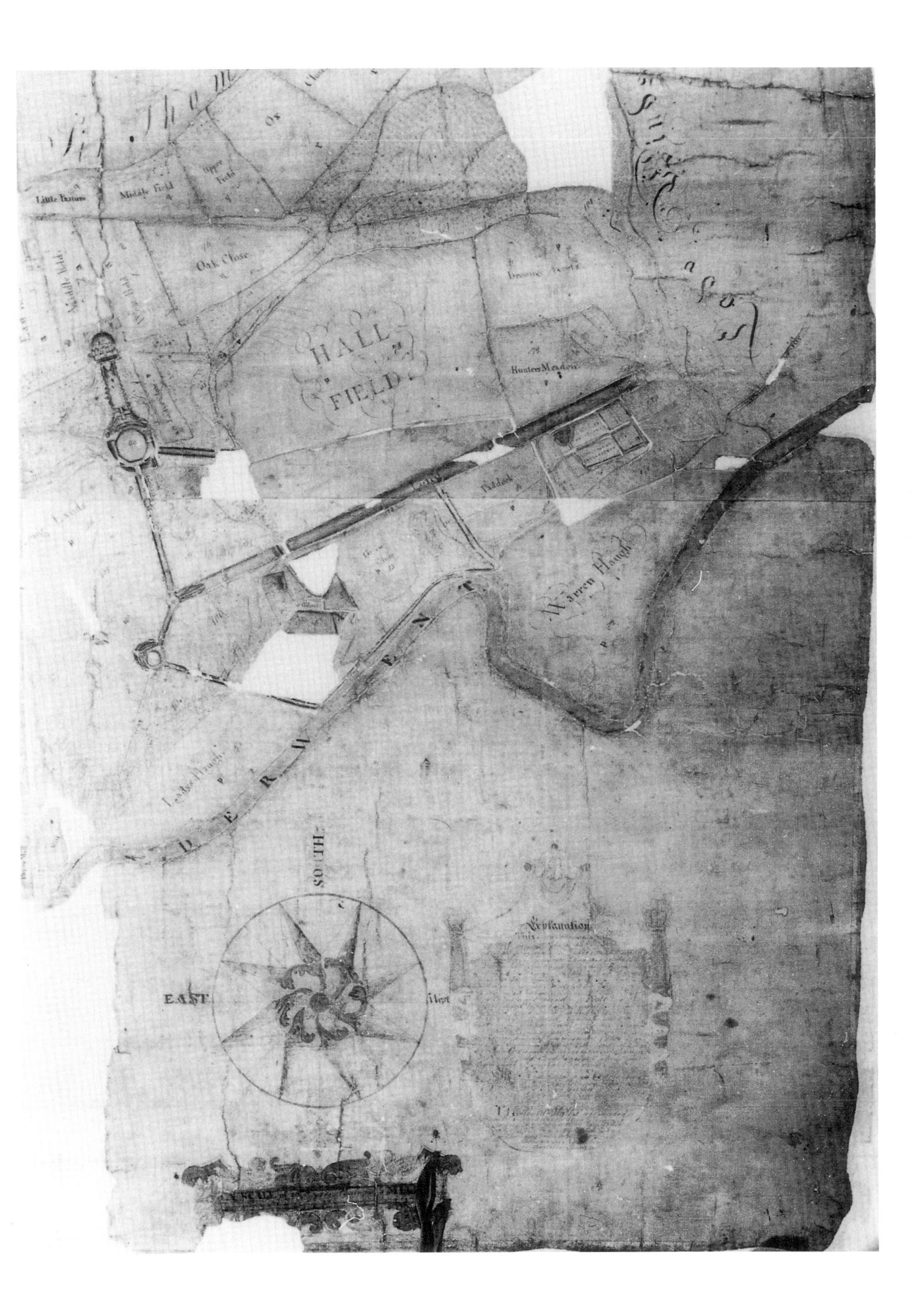
Little Pasture
Middle Field
Upper Field
Middle Field
Oak Close
HALL FIELD
Hunters Meadow
Paddock
Warren Haugh
D E R W E N T
SOUTH
EAST
West
Explanation

## *The Architect for the Chapel*

James Paine was the architect chosen to design the Chapel. Since taking over the completion of the Column to Liberty from Daniel Garrett he had undertaken some decoration at Gibside House, and had built a number of villas in north east England which George Bowes could have visited.

Paine designed a new house at Belford for Abraham Dixon with a central block, flanked by wings for domestic offices and stables in the Palladian style. Only the central block was built about 1756, and was five bays wide and two and a half storeys high. There was an engaged portico above a rusticated basement, with the entrance on the first floor originally reached by a double flight of steps. The enrichment of the southern facade had variety and elegance.[6]

Bywell Hall was designed for William Fenwick slightly later, about 1760. Here the composition of the facade was more complex with a triple-pedimented south front, and the main entrance through the rusticated ground floor. Paine also designed Gosforth Hall for the merchant Sir Charles Brandling. This was the largest villa he had built up to that time. He made the first design in 1755 and building continued until 1764. He designed an even larger mansion in 1758 at Axwell Park, on the opposite side of the Derwent Valley from Gibside. This commission was unsatisfactory for Paine. His client, Sir Thomas Clavering, altered the designs and omitted some ornamentation which Paine had planned.[7]

In addition Paine designed garden buildings for John Burdon at Hardwick near Sedgefield in County Durham. Burdon bought the estate in 1748 and two years later began to lay out the grounds. The terrain was rather flat and featureless, but the buildings notable. A lake, partly surrounded by a serpentine canal, was the central feature of the design, with Paine's garden buildings making it a fine example of the Kentian 'jardin anglais'. Among the buildings Paine designed for Hardwick were a Doric Bath House, a Gothic 'Bona Retiro' or retreat, the Temple of Minerva, square with a peristyle and an octagonal dome, a Gothic gatehouse and a Banqueting House. These were all built in a three year period from 1754 and were richly decorated with plasterwork by Giuseppe Cortese (active *c.* 1725-1778), and paintings in the Banqueting House by Francis Hayman (1708-1776) and Samuel Wale (active 1752-1786). Burdon later went bankrupt from the expense of these buildings, and was unable to carry through the design by Paine of a large mansion for the site.

By now Paine was a skilled and experienced designer of houses, particularly in the villa form. He had spent a year in Italy in 1755-6, taking leave from the Board of Works, but in spite of his tour, he held that as much could be gained from studying books produced when the antiquities were more complete.[8] He had not yet however, designed a free-standing church. A design by Paine for a church in the Palladian style is on loan to the RIBA Drawings Collection from the Victoria & Albert Museum. The drawing resembles S. Giorgio Maggiore, Venice, by Palladio, the engraving of which appeared in volume two of Kent's *Designs of Inigo Jones*. In Paine's design however the interlocking pediment motif is replaced by a central pediment with flanking roofs. A Gibbs' style lantern completes the composition. The drawing is thought to be about 1750. At Cusworth Hall, Yorkshire, Paine was asked to add a chapel and library to a house built eight years before by George Platt (1700-1743) of Rotherham. Paine added single storey pavilions to the south front, with a pediment over a large arched window flanked by niches. At the outer end of each pavilion was a canted bay. Here Paine designed what was virtually a free-standing chapel, though attached to the west of the house. The interior decoration was rich with an Ionic columnar screen framing the altar apse. The plasterwork was by Joseph Rose senior (*c.* 1723-1780) and Christopher Richardson undertook the carving.

James Paine wrote to Bowes from Cavendish Bridge in Derbyshire, where he was building a bridge over the river Trent:

> I am sorry I have not been able ere now to send you the Plans and Sections of the Mausoleum intended under yor. Chapel at Gibside which I hope you will approve of, I think it will be a fine Effect.[9]

His letter was dated 23 June 1760, and it appeared that Paine had already submitted preliminary plans for the chapel to his patron.

## *The building of the Chapel*

Work had begun winning stones for the Chapel in November 1759[10] and in July 1760 digging of the foundations began. George Bowes died of a lingering illness on 17 September 1760 and so only saw the beginning of the building of the Chapel. At this time his daughter, Mary Eleanor, was just eleven, and the responsibility for continuing to build the Chapel fell on the trustees named in Bowes' will. The costs continued to be administered by the estate as before.

At first the main activity was winning stones from nearby quarries and carrying them to the site of the Chapel, then work on the vault beneath began. On 25 July 1761 Joseph Palliser submitted his 'bill four Weeks making Centers for the Arch' and at the beginning of August John Coats junior made 'eight Crooks for the entrance of Vault', these being hinges on which to hang the doors. Masons and labourers worked away at the vault, which was circular with a central pillar and eleven niches for coffins in the outer wall. Later that year Joseph Palliser made doors for the vault and covered it over. Work on the Chapel proceeded slowly in 1762-3. The estate workmen at this time were engaged in repairing the Bath Bank, making a bridge near the Bath, and building a wall with balusters before the Bath House, and in August 1763 Joseph Palliser submitted his bill 'for setting up the Statues at the Bath and Painting them'.[11]

Towards the end of 1764 more active building of the Chapel was resumed, and in November of that year masons and labourers were 'Winning Stones at Wheatleys Quarry for Columns'. George Bowes' fears that his quarries would not yield stone of sufficient length for the chapel's columns proved unjustified, though the quarry was outside the boundaries of the Gibside Estate. The following January Mrs. Bowes 'Paid Mr. Paine his Bill for drawing the Plans for the said Chapel' 50 guineas. Paine had been paid a total of 27 guineas for his work on the Column to Liberty, after he took over from Daniel Garrett. The payment of 50 guineas for plans of the Chapel gives some idea of the amount of work involved. A letter was posted on 5 January 1765 to Christopher Richardson, the carver of the statue of Liberty and other work for Paine. His reply that he would undertake the delicate carving for the Chapel was received on 8 March, and a model sent from his home in Doncaster. The fineness of his carving justified the choice. The working drawings of details for the Chapel were now being made. John Leybourne worked in March 1765 for '1 Day at Gibside drawing the circular Cornice for the Dome, circular architrave, and several other Moulds...'

In March 1765 thirty pieces of Riga Timber, 970 feet in all, were bought from James Norman. These must have been for the strongest load-bearing beams. The following May Andrew Falla and John Leybourne were engaged in mason work at the capitals, and in June the carving began. Meanwhile the interior of the Chapel walls were filled with walling bricks, and by the beginning of July they were 'walling the inside'.

In July 1765 the Gibside Journals record 'Paid Masons scapeling the inside $^1/_2$ and $^1/_4$ Columns Pillasters, and for work at the Festoons'.[12] The delicate work on the engaged pilasters of the domed corners added greatly to the beauty of the Chapel. Scaffolding was provided both inside and outside the Chapel, numerous cramps were made for securing stonework and the filling in of the walls continued. The same month of July the estate shared in the purchase of 787 feet of wainscott plank bought from the Earl of Northumberland, and some of this was used for the Chapel. The carving continued and work was done 'at the Festoons, Capitals and Keystone Trusses'.[13]

Making the Chapel weathertight for winter was the next essential, and the Cash Accounts for 12 September 1765 recorded 'Paid Mr. Bell for 20 Tons of Devonshire blue Slate at three Guineas per Ton' £64. John Leybourne was occupied 'setting the Capitals altring and piecing the high Window Soles [sills] &c'. This presumably refers to the window sills of the Diocletian windows, which were set high in each apse. In

18. Pilaster in Chapel.

November a further ten tons of blue slate was bought from Mr. Bell at the same price as before.

In December 1765 Mrs. Bowes made a payment of £50 to Christopher Richardson 'on Account of Carving', and, as was the custom, made the payment herself. Work continued 'dressing Festoons and Capitals', while Cuthbert Palliser was paid for three weeks work 'taking down Scaffolding, taking down Centers, closing in the end of the Deal Roof'. By the end of 1765 £1,798 11s 1d. had been spent on the Chapel.[14] The time allowed for the building of the Chapel according to Bowes' will was nearly up, and the sum allotted for it had nearly been spent, but Mrs. Bowes wished to fulfil her husband's intentions and the building continued.

The dome, like that built by Wren at St. Paul's Cathedral, was secured by an iron band, 'Paid Mrs. Crowley and Compy. for an Iron Circle got in August 1766 for the Dome' £10 5s 6d.[15] This iron band was made at the local Crowley works, which George Bowes' father had helped by supplying timber for the furnaces when they first came to the area. The bill was not paid until 23 September 1768 when the band had been put in place and duly tested.

Lead was bought for covering the portico in January 1768, and by April Cuthbert Palliser was pulling down the carver's shed and smith's shop. The following June labourers were turfing and repairing the ground about the Chapel, and two little grates were bought for it. Christopher Richardson was still engaged in carving in September 1768. The total sum he earned from this commission was £371 0s 6d.

Unskilled work at the Chapel was undertaken by the estate labourers, who spent a great deal of time winning stones and 'bareing mettle', sometime helped by outside contractors such as Richard Bowman and Partners. Both labourers and masons did a lot of preparatory work before more skilled craftsmen took over. Joseph Palliser, the estate carpenter, was in charge of erecting scaffolding for other workers, as well as the finer carpentry. In June 1765 Cuthbert Palliser took over Joseph's work. John Leybourne did most of the mason work before Christopher Richardson completed the carving, and sometimes gained extra money for 'bargain work'. No individual stuccoists are mentioned. Italo-Swiss plasterworkers usually worked from their own designs, and Paine preferred to use his own, and employ craftsmen from a different background who were willing to fall in with his ideas. Paine therefore used mainly English plasterworkers and there are only four documented instances of him using Italian stuccoists.[16] Philip Daniel was Swiss in origin and had completed the stuccowork at the Banqueting House. He worked on the estate until 1768 but was not involved in work at the Chapel. By this time he was engaged in routine plasterwork at Gibside House and other buildings.

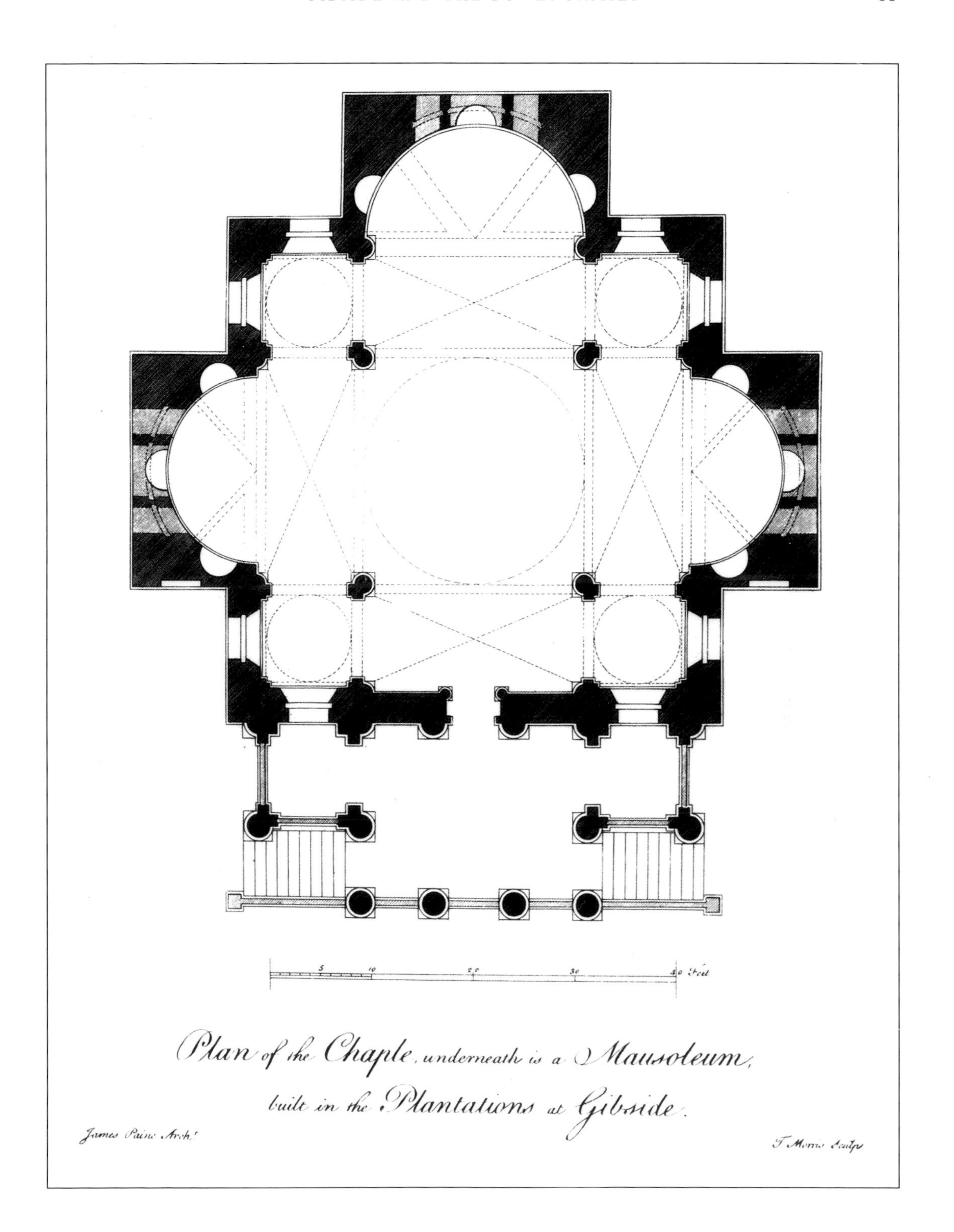
5 10 20 30 40 Feet
Plan of the Chaple, underneath is a Mausoleum,
built in the Plantations at Gibside.
James Paine Arch.t
T Morris Sculp

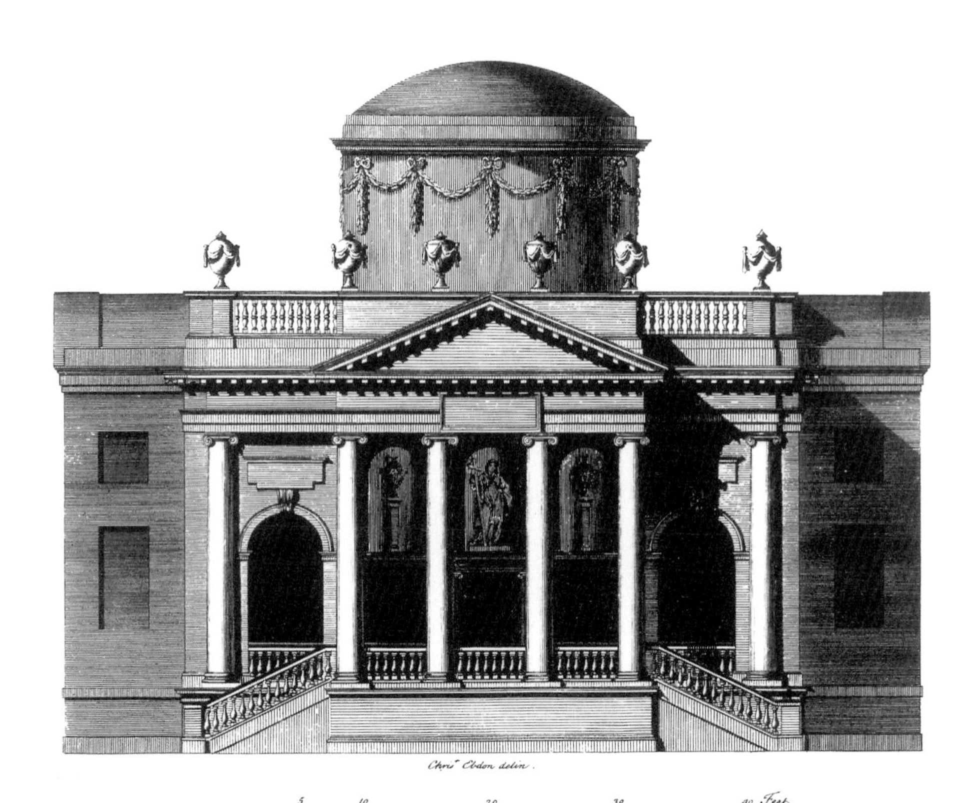


20 and 21. Elevation and Section of Chapel by Paine.

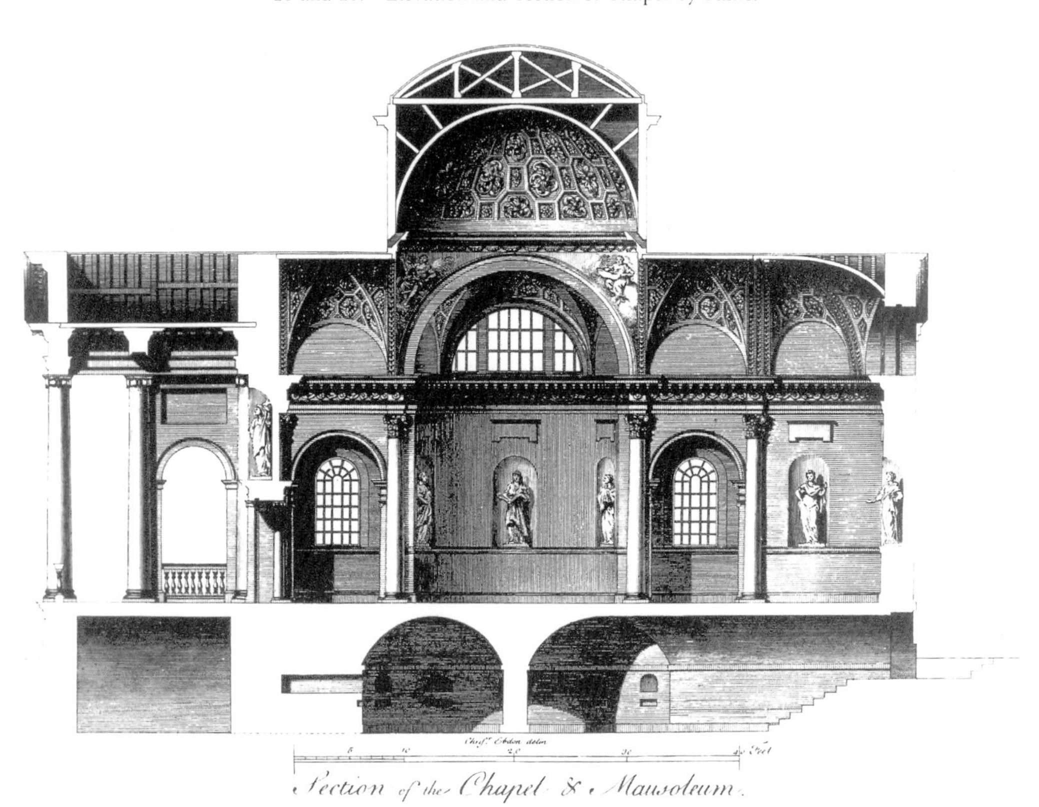

22. Chapel dome with urns.

## *The Chapel*

The plan of the Chapel was a Greek cross with the eastern side flattened to form an entrance. As the Chapel faced along Bowes' Grand Walk the entrance facade was elaborately designed. Six giant engaged Ionic columns lined the entrance facade with a portico of four principal columns. A flight of steps on either side led to the podium on which the Chapel stood, with balusters lining the steps and forming a loggia-like area on either side of the portico. Under the portico the carving of the capitals, friezes and modillions was delicate, crisp and beautiful, and worthy of its carver Christopher Richardson. A shallow dome surmounted a tall drum decorated with festoons. The considerable height of the drum was necessary as otherwise the dome could not be seen in a near view.

The interior of the Chapel had a Georgian simplicity, which on further inspection revealed a more complex form. The Greek cross plan had the arms of the cross curved to form apses on the inside of the Chapel, while remaining square on the outside. The fourth arm of the cross was replaced by the entrance facade. Composite columns supported the crossings and the central dome, while at a lower level engaged Ionic pilasters bore a small dome in each corner between the arms of the cross.

The lightness of the interior was achieved by the use of tall windows at the corners of the Chapel, and by slightly bowed Diocletian windows at a high level, reminiscent of those shown

23. Interior of the Chapel.

in Lord Burlington's *The Fabbriche Antiche of Andrea Palladio* (1730). At the base of the drum supporting the dome, sixteen glazed openings were inserted to illuminate the dome's interior. These glazed openings were referred to in an account from John Leybourne: 'Cutting and Working Stones for the Dome Light holes &c. at Gibside Chapel for Mrs. Bowes from Janry. 4th to and with Janry. 21st 1768.'[17]

The interior of the Chapel was not finished according to Paine's design. The coffering shown in the engraving of the interior of the Chapel was omitted, and the plasterwork above the cornice differed from that shown by Paine. According to his design, niches, both inside and out, had been intended to display statues.

The vault was of the same cream stone as the rest of the Chapel and was described by a 19th century writer thus:

> The mausoleum is underneath the chapel, and is entered by a door on the west side, which opens on a short passage and some steps to a burial vault. This vault is formed by a groined arch, round the sides of which are arranged in a semicircle niches for the reception of the remains of members of the family.[18]

The vault was of concentric rings of stone with four rectangular holes in the walls forming part of a heating system fired originally by a stove beneath the floor of the Chapel portico. A central pillar supported the roof, which was elongated on the west side towards the door. The workmanship of the vault was superb. Its entrance

24. The Chapel and entrance to vault.

was at the foot of a gaunt wall, and just above it a broad string course. The wall was then blank until broken by the gentle outward curve of a Diocletian window, which fitted neatly into a broken pediment.

## *Sources for the Chapel*

Paine's main sources for Gibside Chapel were the buildings of Roman antiquity and the churches of Palladio. Andrea Palladio (1508-1580) was born in Padua, where he was a stone-carver until 1524 when he broke his apprenticeship and fled to Vicenza. Here he gained the attention of Giancarlo Trissino, a local nobleman. Trissino educated a group of young aristocrats and Palladio joined their company. He studied architecture and became well versed in Latin authors. In 1541 he made his first visit to Rome, and went there many times to study both the buildings of Roman antiquity and the Renaissance.[19]

As Palladio's experience grew he designed villas for nobles and merchants, who had lost their fortunes when Venice lost command of the seas, and turned to farming. They wanted a dwelling which would combine living quarters with farm buildings near at hand so that supervision would be easy. The villas usually had a main block with a large central hall and smaller rooms leading from it. The kitchen offices were where possible in the basement, or in wings attached to the main block. Some of these villas were temple-fronted with the porch either laid upon it in relief on the facade, or projecting from or receding into the block. Sometimes arcaded utility wings projected from the villa, as at the Villa Barbaro at

Maser of 1557-8. The temple front had been adapted by Palladio from the newly revealed ruins of Rome. At this time domestic buildings had not yet been excavated and Palladio used the temple facade to give grandeur and magnificence to the house, and to emphasize the entrance.[20]

Palladio did not turn to building churches until the 1560s, largely through the absence of commissions. He had used the temple front for houses, and now he used temple fronts linked, but on different planes, in building churches. In the case of S. Giorgio Maggiore, Venice, of 1565, the main pediment and columns were raised on plinths and the interlocking pediment front was based on the ground.

Paine wrote in the preface to his book *Plans, Elevations and Sections of Noblemen and Gentlemen's Houses* v.I (1767)

> ...we have received some real advantages from Palladio, and other Venetian masters, whose works were studied with great application by our countryman Inigo Jones...

and although he went on to say that houses built on such a plan were ill adapted to the English climate, he acknowledged his debt to Palladio.

Little is known of Paine's travels in Italy in the years 1755-6, but it seems likely that he visited Rome and also saw some of Palladio's works. He had a reverence for Roman architecture: 'It is beyond a doubt that the Romans carried this art to a greater height than any other people'[21] and was familiar with Palladio's *Four Books of Architecture*. The book was published in Venice in 1570 and produced in translation by Paine's early mentor Isaac Ware in 1738.

George Bowes' intention to build a Chapel with a Mausoleum at Gibside must have delighted Paine, for it gave him the opportunity to design a Chapel based on his knowledge of Roman architecture and an appreciation of Palladio's works. The Greek cross in a square was the basis of the design. The Greek cross was one of the earliest forms used for religious buildings, long before the Christian era. It became popular with the Romans, and from the 11th century onwards was a favourite form for many churches in the Balkans and Slavic east. The basic plan was used by Jacopo Sansovino (1486-1570) for San Martino, Venice *c.* 1540, and was a form suitable for small congregations. Humanist architects of the Renaissance, from Alberti (1404-1472) to Palladio, had tried to establish the central plan church – either as a circle or a square – as an acceptable type, but the long-naved church persisted.[22]

In his design for the Tempietto at Maser for the Villa Barbaro, built at the end of his life, Palladio built a chapel based on a Greek cross with a wide portico added to one arm to form an entrance. Here Palladio made 'the improbable union of two contrasting forms, the Greek cross and the domed Pantheon- with-portico, by permitting the dome to be supported and buttressed by wall masses...'[23] At Maser a much larger dome than Gibside was used, which masked the shape of the Greek cross in the exterior view. No freestanding supporting columns were needed in the interior, and the arms of the Greek cross had straight sides with slightly curved ends. The portico covered virtually the whole of the entry facade with a richly decorated pediment, and swags high between the columns of the portico.

In Paine's plan for the Chapel at Gibside there were four supporting columns and the central core was expanded into a cross within a square. Externally he designed a building that was not quite symmetrical with the decoration on the entry front, and the other sides varied by windows and roof-line. The dome was enriched by carved swags and urns surmounted the balustrade above the portico.

A change of emphasis in church liturgy had helped Paine in his choice of the centralized plan. The preacher had become more important than the altar, and attention was focussed upon him. This meant that church plans need no longer be dominated by the long nave leading to the altar, and experiments were made with unusual shapes, such as polygons, ovals, circles and squares.[24]

## *The Church in Landscape*

A change of attitude led the owners of country estates to treat churches not only as religious buildings but as part of the landscape to be exploited for their visual qualities. Lord Bathurst began his improvements at Cirencester Park about 1715. The Broad Avenue, which divided his park into two unequal parts, was aligned with Cirencester Church steeple, while the view from Pope's seat was focussed on the spire of the nearby Kemble Church. At St. Paul's Walden Bury Edward Gilbert, the second Mrs. Bowes' father, added a decorative chancel to the Parish Church in 1727. He also laid out the grounds of his nearby house at the same time and aligned one of the *allées* leading from the lawn to the north of the house with the Parish Church.

In an effort to improve the view from the houses of country landowners, whole villages were moved some distance from their original site. George Bowes had dealt with such a situation when he removed the 'village of Gibside' from an area to the east of Gibside House before he started his improvements in 1729.[25] At Kirkby Fleetham, Yorkshire, a house was built about the 1750s probably for William Aislabie of Studley Royal. The Norman Church of St. Mary was left near the house, while the village was moved a mile away. It formed part of a Palladian landscape which has been ascribed to Daniel Garrett.[26] At Castle Howard, Yorkshire, the old village of Henderskelfe, along with the Parish Church, was destroyed to make way for the new landscape. The Parish Church had been the burial place for the Howards in that area, and only that function of the church was retained on the estate, leading to the building of Hawksmoor's Mausoleum in 1729-36. As well as providing a new family burial place, it made a striking eye-catcher for the park, and a fitting resting place for the 3rd Earl of Carlisle in the landscape he had largely created.[27]

Other landowners rebuilt existing or ruined churches in a classical style to fit in with the rest of their estate. At Aynho, Northamptonshire, the Church of St. Michael was rebuilt in 1725 by Edward Wing, a master builder of Aynho. The medieval tower remained, and next to it rose a substantial building looking more like a Palladian country house than a church. In 1733 the Church of St. Margaret at Well Vale House, Lincolnshire, was rebuilt in the classical style as a *point de vue* from the east front of the house. The church had a portico supported by four thin Tuscan columns echoed by pilasters on the front wall of the church. The plain brick side walls were unbroken save for two tall windows. Insid there was a three-decker pulpit of the same type as that which later furnished Gibside Chapel.

Of those landowners who re-sited villages and churches Simon, 1st Earl of Harcourt, is thought to be responsible for 'The Deserted Village' of Oliver Goldsmith's poem. Lord Harcourt decided to build a Palladian mansion on the banks of the Thames, with a beautiful view of the spires of Oxford. The house was completed in 1760, and in the following year he started to lay out the grounds. The village of Nuneham Courtenay was moved to a site well away from the house. The gravestones in the churchyard were removed and the gravemounds flattened in 1761, while the medieval church remained until at least 1762, the year in which the new Parish Church in the guise of a classical temple was consecrated. On rising ground above the house Lord Harcourt designed the Church of All Saints, aided by James 'Athenian' Stuart (1713-1788). Stuart made corrections to the Earl's design. The Church was completed in 1764. Its plan was a long and irregular rectangle with an apse at either end, and a portico placed away from the entrance on the longer axis of the rectangle. The portico originally concealed a small door, but later this was blocked up. The interior space was not easily adapted for worship, but Lord Harcourt achieved his object in building a domed temple which looked well in the landscape near his house.

Damie Stillman refers to the conflict between religious and secular concerns in the re-siting of church buildings for non- ecclesiastical purposes:

> Although the ostensible purpose of these buildings was to serve as the parish church, their location was often determined not by convenience for the worshippers, but by their role as ornaments in gardens, as *points de vue*, or as symmetrical balances for stables and outbuildings.[28]

He mistakenly gives Gibside as the first of a number of examples. Gibside Chapel was certainly a *point de vue*, but it was not a re-sited church. Bowes did not displace an already established congregation and the Chapel was a new place of worship, built three miles from the Parish Church at Whickham. It was nearer to the homes of many of the estate workers than the Parish Church, and served as a place of worship both for the family at Gibside House, and those on the estate who wished to worship there.

The building of private chapels still occasionally took place in the region, and not necessarily in the fashionable Palladian mode. Chipchase, Northumberland, was bought by John Reed of Bellingham in 1734. He built a new Chapel to replace the medieval one and sited it a short distance away from Chipchase Castle. He was buried in the Chapel he had built in April 1754. The style was plain with the main adornment in the surrounds of the four sash windows on the south side, which were almost domestic in character.

Bowes' private Chapel was similar to Palladio's Tempietto at Maser not only in design, but also in its relationship to the house it served. However at Maser the Tempietto was near the Villa Barbaro and stood in a square on what is now the public highway, while at Gibside the house and Chapel were some distance apart, and within private property. The Chapel was the focal point in Bowes' landscape plan of garden buildings, walks and fine trees, and the culmination of his design for Gibside.

After his death in 1760 building of the Chapel had continued with his wife's supervision. On the marriage of his daughter, Mary Eleanor, in 1767 the question of the completion of the Chapel arose. John Bell (active 1760-*c.* 1785), a Durham architect and builder who often worked with James Paine, surveyed the Chapel in February 1768.[29] This would give an accurate picture of how the building was progressing, and help Mary Eleanor and the trustees of George Bowes' will decide on its future. Up to the end of 1768 over £4,000 was spent on it, more than twice the amount allowed for in George Bowes' will.

Mary Eleanor was now eighteen, and as a young bride her thoughts turned to other things. The Chapel was weatherfast, and decorated up to the cornice, but after two small payments in 1769, no more was spent on the Chapel until it was again surveyed by John Bell in October and November 1775.[30] The survey was completed in the following April, and it may have led to a small repair carried out in November 1776, when Hope & Partners were 'cutting the Lead out for the Plumber at the Chaple'. It was nearly forty years after this survey that the Chapel was at last completed.

CHAPTER
# 7

## MARY ELEANOR BOWES
Countess of Strathmore 1749-1800

# *The Most Intelligent Female Botanist*

### *The Young Heiress*

Mary Eleanor was born when her father was nearly fifty, and perhaps unused to children about the house. She seems to have been treated as a young adult rather than a child, with great attention paid to learning and accomplishments. She could read well at the age of four, and her father's aim was that she should improve her knowledge in any subject for which she showed a talent. Mrs. Bowes' Cash Accounts for 1755 show that at six years old she was taking lessons from drawing and dancing masters at two guineas each a month, while the writing master's charge was one guinea. Later she was taught music by Charles Avison, the composer and celebrated organist of St. Nicholas' Church in Newcastle. Her father thought that her constitution should be hardened in every way possible and she was inoculated against smallpox at the age of three, but he omitted to give her moral instruction, or to teach her forgiveness of others. She became learned, particularly in botany and languages, and wished to write.

Her father, as befitted his position, attended Whickham Church, and one Sunday in the summer of 1756 the bells were rung 'on George Bowes Esqr. and Miss Bowes coming out of Church'. Bowes' attitude to religion is not clear. As a young man he had given two flagons to Whickham Church. In 1748 he subscribed £50 towards the rebuilding of the nearby Tanfield Church, and in 1759 gave money towards the repair of Lamesley Chapel five miles from Gibside. These may merely have been gifts of a public-spirited landowner, though his second wife's fondness for religion must have had some influence upon him.

Bowes was proud of his daughter's knowledge and liked to show her skills to his friends. She learnt speeches from Ovid's *Metamorphoses* and Milton by heart and recited them to gatherings at Gibside. Bowes subscribed to various journals and newspapers in the 1750s, thus making sure Mary Eleanor would have a knowledge of current affairs. They included the *London Magazine, Newcastle General Magazine, Newcastle Intelligencer* and *The Newcastle Courant*. He also subscribed to the *Amsterdam Gazette* to keep abreast of the diamond market. A separate heading in the Gibside Ledgers 'Account of Jewels' was kept up to date, while his account with Child's Bank in London recorded that on 14 May 1730 Bowes retrieved a parcel of jewels which he had deposited there in the previous year. Bowes also bought stock in his daughter's name, and she, together with Bowes himself and his father-in-law, Edward Gilbert, subscribed to the Gibside Whale Fishing Company promoted in 1753.

Mary Eleanor's interest in gardening and botany began early, and in May 1761 Joseph Palliser was 'Palisading Miss Bowes's Garden in the Green-Close'. This was an irregularly-shaped grassy area near the house, encircled by trees on three sides. She was then twelve years old, and according to the calculations of the Gibside agent, William Leaton, a very rich heiress. She had a yearly accumulated income of £7,477 with the prospect of an estate of £100,000, plus timber upon the estate worth £50,000 when she came of age.[1] John Sykes in *Local Records* (1833) reported that on his death in 1760 'Mr. Bowes left an only daughter, Mary Eleanor, heiress to an estate of £600,000'. Other accounts give her an even larger fortune. Her wealth would make Mary Eleanor a very desirable bride when she was of a suitable age to marry.

Mary Eleanor enjoyed children's balls which were given in the area for boys and girls from the ages of five or six to fourteen. She particularly liked those given by the Earl and Countess of Northumberland. Here she met Campbell Scott,

the Duke of Buccleuch's younger brother and they were teased into believing they loved each other by her Liddell cousin. The attachment lasted for a year until Scott joined the army and was sent to Germany where he died of smallpox. Another suitor was Charles James Fox, who had been at Eton with Campbell Scott and Liddell. Mary Eleanor recalled in her *Confessions*[2] that Charles James Fox 'had a great liking for me, and followed me' but saw that she preferred Mr. Scott. When Mary Eleanor was nearly thirteen she and her mother went to London but her mother became ill and left her in London in the charge of her aunt, Jane Bowes. Her aunt had been 'a celebrated beauty and extremely vain' and thought little of being hostess to a niece 'who was one of the greatest fortunes in England; and... a prodigy of learning.' Her aunt was an indulgent chaperone and Mary Eleanor was left much to her own devices.

When at Gibside in October 1763 Mary Eleanor had a narrow escape. Mrs Montagu wrote to Lord Bath telling of 'a horrid plot to run away with Miss Bowes'. A man who was 'a famous pimp at the Cardigan's Head' had been sent to bribe Miss Bowes' footman with £20,000 if he would help to abduct his mistress. A member of Parliament hoped to marry her and thus make his fortune. The footman was the lover of Mary Eleanor's former nurse, who now acted as her maid, and they eventually revealed the plot. Mary Eleanor never knew who she could really trust and had very few true friends. It was a relief when she became acquainted with Mrs. Montagu of Denton Hall whose wit and vitality were well-known and who later became the first 'Blue-Stocking'. Mrs Montagu at this time thought well of Mary Eleanor 'she is real[l]y a fine girl, lively, sensible, and very civil and good natured.' Unfortunately Mary Eleanor lacked judgement and had a taste for the romantic which led to unhappy results.

25. Portait of Mary Eleanor Bowes, miniature by J.C.D. Engleheart after George Engleheart.

Meanwhile her mother carefully maintained the Gibside estate and the buildings erected in her father's time were well cared for. The Bath Bank and the Bath House above it were renovated, the floodgates on the River Derwent and the water wheel of the Paper Mill by the river were repaired, while the Warren and Bath Quays bordering the estate were made good. Trees were replaced and tended, and the practice of lighting fires regularly in the Bath and Banqueting Houses was continued. In 1764 part of Gibside House was re-roofed and various rooms redecorated.

Many suitors wished for the hand of Mary Eleanor, who was heiress to such great wealth and estates. Lord Lyttleton wrote to Mrs. Montagu about George Bowes shortly after his death:

> As his vanity descends with his estate to his daughter, I don't wish to see her my daughter-in-law, though she would make my son one of the richest and consequently, in our present ideas of greatness, one of the great peers of the Realm.[3]

Mary Eleanor enjoyed life in London 'with alternate study and diversions', and danced frequently at Almack's Assembly Rooms with Lord Mountstuart and Mr. Chalenor as her most regular beaux. There was a great uproar when the two men nearly fought a duel over who was to sit next to her for supper at Almack's. The poet Thomas Gray reported that 'it is sure the lady did refuse both Lord Mountstuart and the Duke of Beaufort'. The choice finally fell on John Lyon, 9th Earl of Strathmore and Kinghorn, whose mother was the daughter of James Nicholson of West Rainton in the County of Durham. Part of his boyhood had been spent in Durham County, he was twelve years older than Mary Eleanor, handsome and with a good education. Following the death of the 8th Earl of Strathmore in 1753 the 4th Earl of Chesterfield wrote to a friend about his kinsman, the 9th Earl:

> The present Lord is seventeen, a good classical scholar, and with a turn on learning. At this age Lady Strathmore will probably think it proper to send him either to an university or to travel: and if to an university, I should much prefer an university in Scotland to either of ours here.[4]

1762

His mother, however, had friends who advocated that Lord Strathmore should be sent to Pembroke College, Cambridge, as were her two younger sons. Later he travelled abroad with Thomas Pitt, nephew of William Pitt, 1st Earl of Chatham, and they wrote a journal of their travels to Portugal and Spain in 1760. The marriage with Mary Eleanor must have been decided upon by June 1766, when Lord Chesterfield wrote to the Duke of Newcastle about his kinsman. Lord Strathmore had asked to be recommended to the Duke to be one of the sixteen peers of Scotland, in place of Lord Sutherland, who had recently died. Chesterfield advised him:

> to lay before the Administration a particular of Miss Bowes's fortune and of the influence that always accompanies such immense properties[5]

and that this could be his best solicitor.

Mary Eleanor was at first much attracted to Lord Strathmore whose good looks had led to him being known as 'The Beautiful'. Her mother opposed the marriage and thought her daughter would refuse him. There were three objections made by Mrs Bowes which were recounted in Mary Eleanor's *Confessions:* 'disorder in the family; a mother, and many brothers and sisters, whom, perhaps, I should find troublesome; and lastly (the chief with her) his being a Scotchman.' Mary Eleanor countered that the first objection was a false report made through jealousy, that she would like a large family and she was more partial to the Scots and the Irish than the English. However in the one and a half years it took to draw up the marriage settlement her doubts grew. She wrote that 'I found our tempers, dispositions, and turns different' but her pride would not let her admit her mistake. There was delay over Lord Strathmore taking the name of Bowes, as required in her father's will, as well as financial matters to be arranged.

Shortly before Lord Strathmore's marriage with Mary Eleanor Lord Chesterfield wrote to his son:

> My kinsman, Lord Strathmore, is to be married, in a fortnight, to Miss Bowes, the greatest heiress, perhaps, in Europe, and ugly in proportion.[6]

The couple were married on Mary Eleanor's 18th birthday 24 February 1767, at St. George's, Hanover Square. They lived partly in the country at Gibside and partly in London. The following summer Thomas Gray, who had known Lord Strathmore at Pembroke, wrote to his friend and biographer, William Mason:

> tomorrow I go *vizzing* to Gibside to see the New-married Countess, whom (bless my eyes!) I have seen here already.[7]

Jesse Foot, a surgeon who became involved with the family, and later wrote a book about them, described Lord Strathmore as 'a sincere friend, a hearty Scotchman, and a good bottle companion'. He did not however mention that Lord Strathmore was a good scholar, or the improvements made to his estate at Glamis during his ownership. Their first child, Lady Maria, was born 23 April 1768, and a week later John Spragge received half a guinea 'for Ringing on the News of Lady Strathmore being deliver'd'. Thomas Gray wrote to James Brown, later Master of Pembroke:

> I saw my Ld & Tom the other day at breakfast in good health, & Lady Maria did not beat me, but giggled a little.[8]

Mary Eleanor came of age on 24 February 1770, and the event was celebrated shortly afterwards:

> On account of Lady Strathmore's coming of age, a great entertainment was given at his lordship's seat, at Gibside, to a number of gentlemen in the two counties. An ox was roasted whole, which with other victuals and some hogsheads of strong ale, &c., were given to the populace, many hundreds having assembled there to celebrate the day. The house was open for ten days to all persons who chose to repair thither to regale themselves. His lordship's agent gave a genteel entertainment in Newcastle, to the people employed in his service in that town and neighbourhood. Ringing of bells and other demonstrations of joy were likewise shewn on the occasion.[9]

26. Portrait of John, 9th Earl of Strathmore, by Nathaniel Dance, 1762.

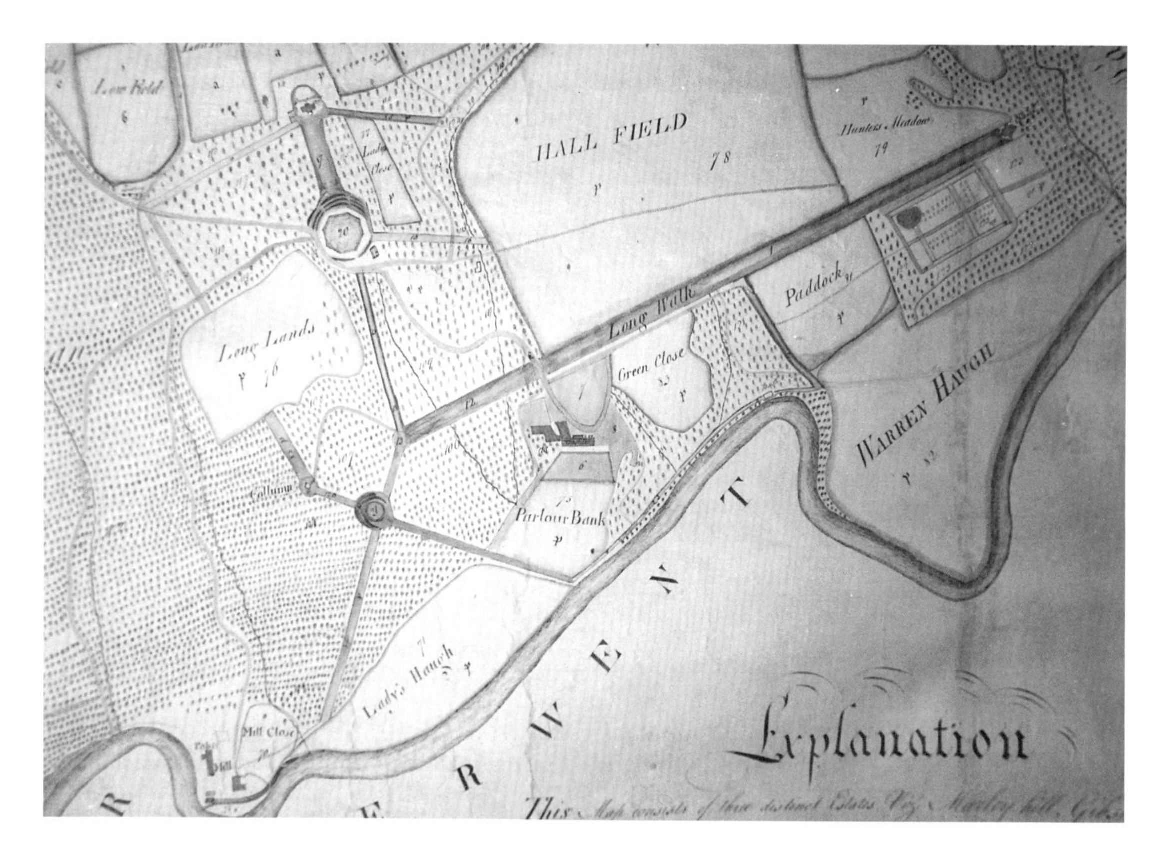


Map 5 Gibside, from copy of 1767 map, detail of central area and House. North at the foot of the map.

Mary Eleanor and her husband were not ideally suited. He was easy- going and amiable, and she was given to quickly-changing enthusiasms and prejudices, but five children were born of the marriage, and the estate at Gibside prospered.

## *The Green House*

Mary Eleanor, having fulfilled her father's wishes by finishing Gibside Chapel as far as seemed reasonable, turned to a project very dear to her heart, that of building a greenhouse at Gibside. The building was started in February 1772, when the first reference was made in the Cash Accounts to the 'New Green House'.[10] Its site was at the top of a steep bank above the water meadow at Warren Haugh. Switzer had advised that a greenhouse should be built with a south wall declining 20° to the east. The tall windows of the south east facade looked on to a paddock where an ornamental pond 50 feet across was made, while the rear of the building had smaller windows because of its exposed position. Magnificent views could be seen of the River Derwent and the surrounding countryside. It was a handsome building, placed on a podium and rectangular in shape, save for the canted bay at the rear, and measured 60 feet x 40 feet 9 inches. It was faced in ashlar, and the stone came from various quarries on or near the estate. Hand-made brick was used in the interior, with a lath and plaster finish.

The building has been attributed to James Paine on stylistic grounds, but with no documentary evidence. It does not appear in the two volumes which illustrated his works. The first volume of 1767 was too early to record it, and either he chose not to include it in volume two of 1783, or it was not his work. The plan does however bear a distinct relationship to the Temple of Diana at Weston Park, Staffordshire, which was designed by James Paine and built 1765-70, two years before the Green House at Gibside was begun. The plan of the Temple of Diana is more complex, but if the Weston Park Temple were extended over the podium on either side of the building, it would approximate to the shape and size of the Gibside Green House, including the canted bay at the back. The oval room at the front of the Temple at Weston Park was designed as a greenhouse, with three tall windows facing across the park, and an identical window at right angles on each side. Ionic columns divided the windows and these projected for more than half of the column drum before the insertion of the window recess, in the same way as at Gibside. In the engravings of Paine's drawings for the Temple of Diana urns adorn the balustrade over each column. At Weston Park these have long since vanished, and at Gibside the remaining urns have now been removed.

Stephen Switzer wrote in *Ichnographia Rustica* (1718) of a greenhouse:

> The Outside is built of the finest Stone, adorn'd with numerous Columns of the finest Architecture, and the main Front neatly set off with extensive Sash Windows, in Height almost from the Bottom to the Top.

The most important feature of the Gibside Green House was the windows, which were large and elaborate. The arcade which fronted the building consisted of seven bays of Tuscan columns. Each column projected over half its width on either side of the 7½ inch gap left for the sash window. These windows formed a double square, plus a semi-circular top, sliding vertically on pulleys. To the rear were two entry doors leading to draught lobbies to maintain an even temperature within. These doors had handsomely detailed pediments, and a semi-circular window above opening inwards. The two windows on the sides of the Green House were the same height and general pattern as those on the facade, but rather narrower. The window design had been scientifically calculated to give both optimum light and temperature. The five windows at the rear of the building faced north east and were small to keep out the elements. As at Weston Park there was no glass in the roof, but a shallow hipped roof of slate was masked by a balustrade decorated with urns. This construction meant that all light had to be provided by windows, and as the width of the building was two thirds that of its length, useful light could not reach the centre of the building. The Green House may have been divided by either a wall or screen, forming a separate room at the rear between the two draught lobbies. To make the greatest use of light a wooden display stage for plants was constructed by the carpenter in the middle of the Green House. Another solution would have been a glass roof, but although this had been used at Chatsworth at that time, it was not yet common.

The small entry lobbies had walls reaching to the full height of the Green House. They prevented draughts reaching delicate plants and were of slightly differing shape. The one near Gibside House was oval and had a fireplace and four decorative wall niches. It would have made a comfortable room for those approaching from Gibside House before they entered the Green House itself. The lobby on the Chapel side was rectangular with rounded corners and contained the heating system for the building. Part of the floor was excavated to hold a boiler and furnace and a central vaulted area was used as a coal store. There was not much space to store fuel, but the estate was rich in timber and coal and deliveries could be made directly if needed. Alterations made to the Green House in the middle of the nineteenth century make interpretation of the original structure difficult. The building is now ruinous, though the arcade facade still has a handsome appearance.

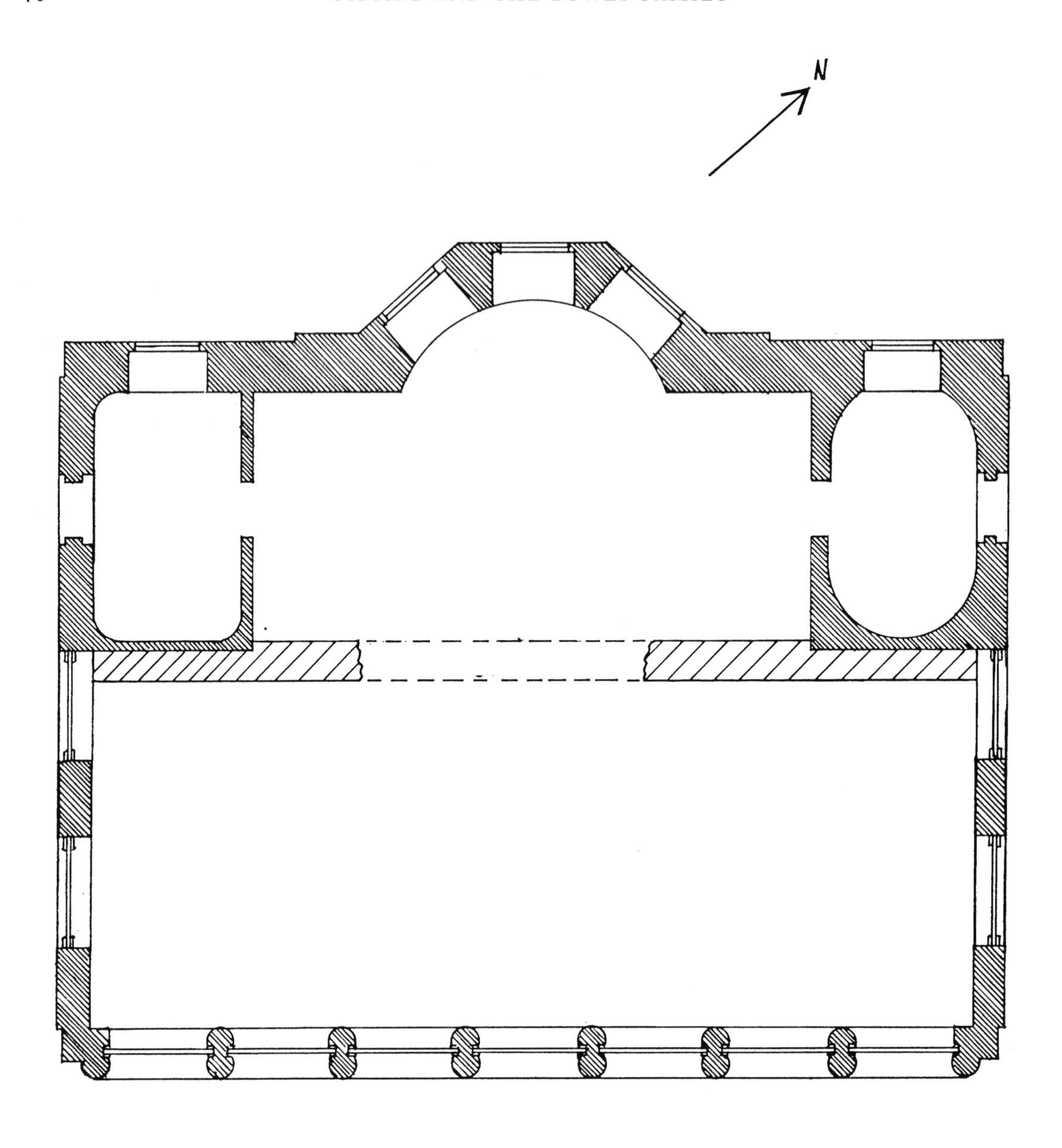


27. Plan of Green House.

28. The Green House, ?early twentieth century.

## *The building of the Green House*

Building began in February 1772 and in the following months stone for the Green House was quarried at East Wood and West Wood Quarries on Gibside Estate, and Crook Gate and Wheatley's Quarries to the south. Flags were got from Friarside Quarry, and mettle came from Busty Bank Quarry. In April 1772 Cuthbert Palliser was paid £1 10s 10s for 'making a shade, [shed]. Rolls and Mells for the Masons', and in July of that year George Harrison and Richard Relph were paid for dressing slates. The next month labourers were paid for 'watching the Green House two Sundays and at the brick kiln & at Wheatley's Quarry' £1 1s. Vandalism which had previously occurred in June 1768, was again a threat.

By the beginning of October 1772 Cuthbert Palliser had been working 'at the Green House Sashes, making Centers, Moulds, putting up Scaffolds, sawing Wood, for the Roof & to the Roof' £6 5s 4d.[11] In November George Robson was paid for burning lime, and four days later hair was bought, as if in preparation for plaster work. A large number of slates were bought for the Green House at the end of 1772, and also 'Deals, Balks Wainscott boards' to the value of £105 13s 10d.

Cuthbert Palliser was making sash frames and working at the Green House roof in January 1773, and in March George Harrison's 'Bill of days work at Crook gate quarry, cutting holes in ye Cornice for the Plummers' £3 1s 4d. was paid. At the beginning of April William Dixon made 'five semicircular ribbits for the windows at the Green House'.[12] This was smith's work and cost £2 1s. As five windows only are mentioned it must have been for the five windows at the back of the building. John Grey supplied sash cord in June 1773, at a cost of £4 16s., so the windows must have been nearing completion. Fundamental building, however, was still in progress in July:

> By The new Green House Paid George Harrison's Bill of days work wheeling Mettle

29. The Green House arcade, 1993.

> to the Landing of the steps, raising the Floor, cutting out of the building drains Levelling them up again, weighing up the Green House Floor, putting in screw Bolts, and for days works at Crookgate Quarry £9 5s 1d.[13]

Francis Dent was paid £30 10s on August 11 'on acct. of glazing'. There was a further instalment of eight guineas in September, and Dent's glazing account was completed in November with a payment for £6 16s. Joseph Barrass provided sash pulleys, and lead was supplied by Sir Walter Blackett, who was paid 'in full for Lead for the Green House' £112 12s 9d.[14] The furnace was set in place by George Harrison at the cost of 3s 6d., and furnace bars added later. He was also paid for 'mason work at the Vases', to prepare them for the finer work of carving, which was carried out by Richard Stephenson at 3 guineas for each vase. Cuthbert Palliser built wooden staging to display plants in December 1773, and later made shelves to fit it. He also made a wooden floor for the Green House, and in June 1774 the stage was painted by Henry Smith. He did further painting in November 1774:

| | |
|---|---|
| Henry Smith Painting the Stage | 6.1.3 |
| painting seven windows inside and out | 2.2.0 |
| and five windows at the backside 10s. | 8.13.3[15] |

In December 1774 Robert Carr supplied '7 large tubbs for Orange Trees' justifying the modern name of Orangery. This provided an orange tree for each of the seven windows of the Green House arcade. In the same month Richard Stephenson was paid £14 11s 6d. 'on account of Carving of the Green House vases', work on which he had begun the previous June. In December 1775 payments for the vases were concluded by a sad entry:

> By The Green House. Paid James Stephenson the Balance of his Brother's Account for Carving the Vases. 10 at £3. 3. 0 P [er] piece.
>
> Recd. on acco £21. 3s remains £10 3s od[16]

The building of the Green House took two years from 1772-4. The final payment for the vases may have been made later because of Richard Stephenson's death. In June 1776 there were repairs made to the road leading to the Green House, and various entries appear in the Cash Accounts for putting up shelves, buying plants and 'Green House potts', and by February 1778 'repairing the Green House roof'. The stove needed attention and the Green House had to be watched to see that it was not vandalised. The Green House had now become an integral part of the estate.

30. South West entrance of the Green House.

## *Alterations to Gibside House*

With the building of the Green House progressing well, Mary Eleanor wished to alter Gibside House to make it more suitable for her growing family. The birth of Maria Jane in 1768 was followed by that of John in 1769, Anna Maria in 1770, George in 1771 and Thomas in 1773. Although not a dedicated mother Mary Eleanor felt that some changes to the house were necessary. The alterations began in the year of Thomas' birth, and were first mentioned in the Cash Accounts on 14 April 1773, when the labourers were paid for 'digging & wheeling out the Foundations of the New Building'. The alterations were to the East Wing, where yet another attempt was made to provide more useful domestic offices for the house. Work on the foundations continued into July, and by September Cuthbert Palliser was 'making a shade [shed] for the Masons in the Back yard'. The following month George Harrison took down the dairy and began building a bakehouse and a new dairy. New provision was also made for a laundry and wash house. In May 1774 centres to support arches or vaults were made and set up, together with scaffolding. This work, and the laying of joists, continued into July, and 50 tons of blue slates were delivered in September. Three and a half tons of new sheet lead were used in December to roof the new building, and the slating began. Door cases and sashes were put in place and plaster work carried out. The work was continued in April 1775 when Cuthbert Palliser was:

> making Sashes, puttg. in sashes, window Lintles, putting in window seats, putting

31. The Green House from Gibside Sketch Book.

> beads round the Windows, and Chimneys, and making thrisels [thresholds] £11 18s.[17]

Gantries were made for the cellar, and new cellar doors hung. In August 1776 George Handby, the plumber, was 'Laying Pipes to the Back Kitchn. and through the Walls to the New Building', and also altering the gutters on the house. The new wing included a steward's room, a dressing room, and a back kitchen with cellars and brewhouse beneath, as well as the usual kitchen offices. The engraving of the estate made by Bailey in 1782 shows a long three-storey building with a two storey section to the east. This must be the new wing. The building is plain and severe, standing out amongst its surrounding trees.

Mary Eleanor built a new hot house for forcing plants in 1774, when the Green House was nearly finished. Together with the alterations to Gibside House of 1773-6 this was her contribution to new building on the estate.

★ ★ ★ ★ ★

Her family was now complete. However the children did not seem to draw their parents together, for Mary Eleanor favoured her daughters, and took an unjustified dislike to her eldest son. The Earl enjoyed country life. He kept cocks, and paid Sir Blakiston Conyers regular sums for their upkeep, amounting to nearly £200 in 1775. He attended the races, reared partridges

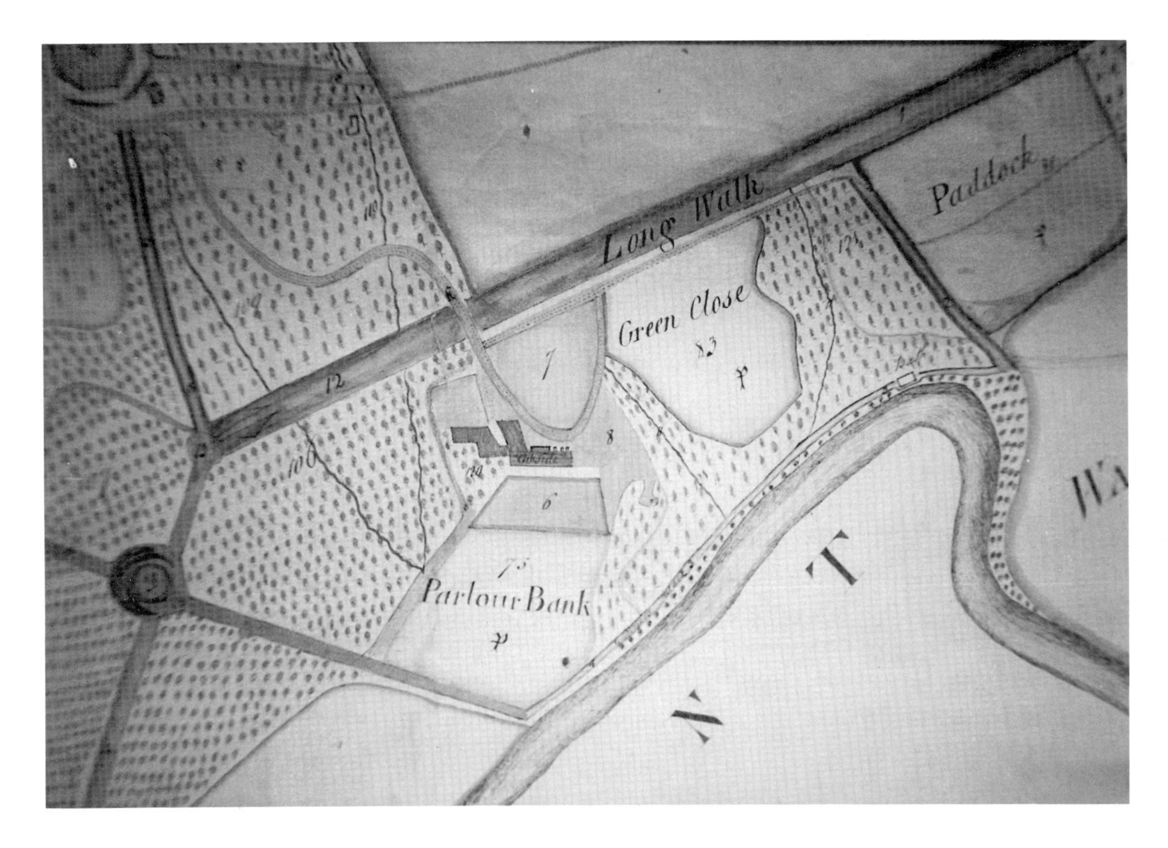


Map 6 Detail of Gibside House from copy of 1767 map.
North at foot of plan.

and was of an amiable disposition. He was not a suitable husband for Mary Eleanor in that he could not sympathise with her passion for writing and botany, or in more serious matters keep her in check. Jesse Foot in *The Lives of Andrew Robinson Bowes Esq., and the Countess of Strathmore* (1810) described her first husband:

> The Earl was not exactly calculated to make even a good learned woman a pleasing husband. His Lordship's pursuits were always innocent and without the smallest guile, but they were not those of science or any other splendid quality... He would rather suffer himself than sour the Countess by imposing any restraints upon her; hence were seen all the learned domestics which haunted his house even in his life-time.[18]

Of Mary Eleanor Jesse Foot wrote:

> Her judgement was weak, her prudence almost none, and her prejudice unbounded. But there was intellect, of that sort which required to be under the control of some other.[19]

In 1776, after a marriage lasting nine years, Lord Strathmore developed consumption. He was on ship en route for Lisbon to effect a cure, when he died on 7 March 1776.

Mary Eleanor was now free of any restraint, and indulged her passion for botany and writing to the full. Jesse Foot called her 'the most intelligent female botanist of the age'. She bought Stanley House in upper Chelsea and built 'extensive hot-houses and conservatories... She had purchased a fine old mansion with extent of ground, well walled in, and she brought exotics from the Cape'.[20] Her garden was not far from the Apothecaries' Garden at Chelsea, which specialised in exotic plants. Mary Eleanor may have been trying to emulate the garden founded by Sir Hans Sloane, and which he gave to the Worshipful Company of Apothecaries in 1722. She commissioned William Paterson, a botanist and traveller, to find her rare and exotic plants, and became friendly with Daniel Carl Solander, a Swedish botanist who had been a protégé of Linnaeus. Solander accompanied his friend and patron Joseph Banks on Captain James Cook's voyage in the 'Endeavour' from 1768-1771 when the east coast of Australia was discovered and New Zealand circumnavigated. On their return they presented the Apothecaries' Garden at Chelsea with seeds from the new continent, and later Solander became Banks' secretary and librarian. He became keeper of the Natural History department at the British Museum in 1773. He was agreeable but indolent and gathered a circle around him which included some of Mary Eleanor's household. Pretending to be Mary Eleanor's friends they took advantage of her hospitality and her wish to hold a 'salon'.

In the biography of Mary Eleanor and her second husband, Andrew Robinson Stoney, Jesse Foot gave a detailed description of Mary Eleanor:

> The Countess at this time was scarcely thirty years of age: she possessed a very pleasing *enbonpoint:* her breast was uncommonly fine; her stature was rather under middle class; her hair brown; her eyes light, small, and she was near sighted; her face was round; her neck and shoulders graceful; her lower jaw rather under-hanging... her fingers were small, and her hands were exceedingly delicate. She appeared in very fine health, her complexion was particularly clear...

and also listed her property:

> The Countess's possessions then were, her house and garden at Chelsea, with conservatories and hothouses; upon the largest scale, her house in Grosvenor Square, her seat at Paul's Walden, Gibside, Streatlam Castle, and Barnard Castle, besides lands in Middlesex.

As an only child she had been spoilt, and now that she lacked the restraints formerly provided by her family, she was a prey to flatterers and fortune-hunters. She had an affair with a Mr. George Grey, was expecting his child, and seemed likely to marry him when she suddenly married an Irishman, Andrew Robinson Stoney, a former army lieutenant, on 17 January 1777. Jesse Foot relates in his *Lives:*

> The person of Bowes was rather in his favour, and his address was, probably, when young, captivating. His speech was soft, his height more than five feet ten... His smile was agreeable, his wit ready, but he was always the first to laugh at what he said, which forced others to laugh also. His conversation was shallow, his education was bare, and his utterance was in a low tone and lisping.[21]

He gained his bride by appealing to her romantic sensibilities with a faked duel on her behalf. The marriage was referred to in a letter from George Selwyn, a member of Parliament, to Lord Carlisle, 'this match of that lunatic's, Lady Strathmore, with Mr. Stoney does indeed present no pleasant prospect to me'.[22]

Apart from being precipitate the match was ill-advised, for Stoney had already married one coal-heiress, Hannah Newton of Cold Pig Hill, to the South of Gibside near Lanchester, and treated her with great cruelty. His mistreatment caused her death, and he now sought a greater prize. Disregarding this, the only safeguard Mary Eleanor made was a settlement of the estates willed to her by her father, so that the rents and produce came to her, whether married or single. This settlement could be revoked by her alone. It meant that her property did not automatically belong to her husband on marriage as decreed by law at that time, and was also designed to look after the welfare of her children.

32. Caricature of Stoney Bowes.

In November 1776, two months before the marriage of Mary Eleanor and Stoney, a notice appeared in The Newcastle Courant:

BUILDING MATERIALS
To be SOLD to the best Bidder,
On Wednesday the 27th of November inst.
at Gibside, in the County of Durham.

Several Tons of Blue Slates; a large quantity of very fine Flags, many of which are polished, and several fothers of very good Quarry Stones, fit for the front of an elegant building, dressed ready for use; also a number of 1 and 2 inch deals, and other Fir Timber; with many other articles, late the property of the Earl of Strathmore, deceased.-

The sale to begin at nine o'clock.

Mary Eleanor, although reputed to have been the richest heiress in Europe, was short of money. Some of the Strathmore estates in Scotland had to be sold after her husband's death, and at the time of her second marriage she was considerably in debt.

On their marriage Stoney took the name of Bowes in accordance with George Bowes' will. Shortly after the wedding Bowes unsuccessfully stood as a member of Parliament for Newcastle. Within ten months of his marriage Bowes was cutting down trees at Gibside. Timber on the estate had been valued at £50,000 shortly after George Bowes' death in 1760. Stoney Bowes wrote of the estate's valuable plantations, 'Such wood is not in England, at least in any one place, his Majesty's Docks excepted'.[23] Some buyers were discouraged as they were uncertain whether he really owned the timber, and he felled more trees than the market would take.

Cold Pig Hill, the property Bowes had inherited from his first wife, was added to the Gibside husbandry records. Lady Strathmore and her husband ate more richly than previous Gibside households:

> paid for Turkeys, Chickens, Butter, Cream, Salmon, Eggs, Pidgeons, Oranges, Apples and Letters [lettuce] for Mr. Bowes and the Countess.

Bowes also had taste for fine dress and 'Anthony Johnson's Bill for Hatts Gold Lace and Stockings &c.' from before the marriage was paid by the estate. A daughter was born to them, and this was celebrated in many anchors of ale.

His extravagance and gaming debts led him in 1779 to sell his wife's house in upper Chelsea with its exotic plants and conservatories. In 1780 Stoney Bowes became sheriff of Northumberland, and once again stood for Parliament. This time he was successful, winning by a margin of 50 votes. 'Bowes is not the kind of colleague that a man would wish for' wrote Nicholas Ridley, brother of the other successful candidate for Newcastle, Sir Matthew White Ridley.[24] Bowes made a show of entertaining those with political influence, and wished for an Irish peerage, but with no success. As a member of Parliament he could not be prosecuted for debt, which was advantageous to him.

Records for Stoney Bowes' time at Gibside are sparse. The series of Cash Accounts ended abruptly on 28 September 1781, and were not resumed until January 1791. If such records were kept they may have been destroyed as giving too accurate an account of his depredations. Gibside was no longer open to visitors as it had been. As long ago as October 1756 an article in *The Newcastle Journal* had remarked 'it is the Pleasure of People of Taste in the North to pay an annual Visit to Gibside Woods'. By 1779 the situation had changed, and Henry Smith, who in happier days had painted the windows and stage in the Green House, had to apply his talent to other things:

> By Repairs & Improvements. Paid Henry Smith Painting and Lettering six Boards of no Road this Way, to put up in the Foot Paths about the Walks at Gibside. 6s.[25]

Access to Gibside was denied, and work to maintain the estate was curtailed. Enterprises begun in George Bowes' time were allowed to die. The Paper Mill by the River Derwent, which had been rebuilt in 1728, was destroyed in 1780 after a dispute between the tenant and Stoney Bowes.

Bowes had caused his first wife's death by his mistreatment, and soon he began to persecute Mary Eleanor. A son was born to them in 1782, but Bowes did not cease his cruelty and attempts to degrade his wife. He used the daughters from her first marriage as pawns in some of his schemes to persecute her. Mary Eleanor feared for her life and while in London in February 1785 she escaped from what had become imprisonment by Bowes. She appealed to the Courts for the restitution of her property and instituted proceedings for divorce against Bowes on the grounds of his adultery. A year later Mary Eleanor gained a judgement against Bowes and he was directed to pay her £300 a year alimony.[26] Bowes saw that if Mary Eleanor obtained her divorce he would lose Gibside with its rents. He determined to abduct his wife and persuade her to live with him once more, dropping her case against him. On November 10th 1787 he suceeded in abducting Mary Eleanor and the next eleven days were spent in a wild venture to the north of England, Streatlam and the moors. They travelled at first by carriage and then on horseback. If questioned Bowes said that his wife was ill or deranged. At Harlow Hill in Northumberland the friends Bowes expected did not appear and they went on to Newcastle. By the 21st November Mary Eleanor was back in London, frail and exhausted. After much misery Mary Eleanor obtained a divorce in 1789. In return for a pension she made over her life interest in Gibside to her eldest son, John, 10th Earl of Strathmore, whom she now valued and respected. She went to live in Christchurch, Hampshire and died there on 28 April 1800. Stoney Bowes was imprisoned for debt, and until the death of Mary Eleanor was confined in the King's Bench prison. Later he was permitted to live outside the prison but 'within the prison rules' until his death in 1810. To the end he continued to scheme to try to improve his lot and deceived anyone who cared for him.

CHAPTER

8

# JOHN BOWES
## 10th Earl of Strathmore 1769-1820

# *A Careful Steward*

### *Man of Taste*

An unidentified traveller in 1789 wrote:

> From Newcastle I made a pleasing Excursion to Gibside, the delightful seat of the Countess of Strathmore, situated on the river Darwen; no Man of the least Feeling can see this charming Place without being sensibly affected with the rapid desolation everywhere taking Place around it, yet it has even now, after 9 years Neglect, sufficient majesty to engage the Attention of every Traveller fond of romantic Scenery.[1]

The traveller found Gibside impressive even in its neglected state. For the young John Bowes, 10th Earl of Strathmore, it must have had a similar attraction, with the added knowledge that it was his inheritance.

After a neglected childhood, with his mother lavishing attention on his sisters, the 10th Earl was sent to various boarding schools, then to Pembroke College, Cambridge, his father's college, and proceeded M.A. in 1786. He then served in the army becoming a captain in the 64th Foot in May 1789. On his majority he decided to give up the army and live at Gibside. He came to an arrangement with his mother, Mary Eleanor, to buy her life interest in Gibside and Streatlam in return for an allowance.

When he took over the Gibside estate it had suffered from despoilment and neglect. His stepfather, Stoney Bowes, had stripped the banks and denes of timber to pay his debts. Some of the estate workers were paid off in 1782, when records were either destroyed or no longer kept. During this time there was a systematic squandering of the assets of the estate. When Mary Eleanor finally obtained a divorce from her second husband in 1789, she was too exhausted to think of restoring the estate. For her son it was his patrimony and he wished that Gibside should once more become what his grandfather had intended – a place of interest and delight.

A friend who lived at Hamsterley Hall near Gibside was Henry Swinburne, son of Sir John Swinburne III of Capheaton, Northumberland. Swinburne took him to see a performance at Seaton Delaval of the *Fair Penitent* given by the family of Lord Delaval, formerly Sir John Hussey Delaval, at Christmas 1790. Lord Delaval, in exchange for maintaining him for life, obtained possession of the family home at Seaton Delaval from his spendthrift brother Francis. His great business acumen caused his enterprises at Seaton Sluice to prosper. He was also a great lover of amateur theatricals, and the heroine of the *Fair Penitent* was his youngest daughter, the lovely Sarah Hussey Delaval, wife of Lord Tyrconnel. The theme of the play was appropriate. Lady Tyrconnel had been on intimate terms with the Duke of York and the affair had now come to an end. The Duke had been forced into a political marriage with a German princess, and Lady Tyrconnel wanted to show she had renounced the Duke's love.

The *Newcastle Chronicle* enthused about her performance in the play:

> Language cannot describe the bewitching charms of the beautiful Calista. The most perfect judgement, taste and elegance characterised this amiable and accomplished female who is the darling of her family and deservedly the admiration of all this part of the world

Lord Strathmore fell deeply in love with Sarah. She was an assured beauty of great charm, six years his senior. He was twenty-one, of a romantic disposition, and immediately attracted by her and the carefree life at Seaton Delaval.

33. Portrait of John, 10th Earl of Strathmore, by Mather Brown.

Sarah could easily get her own way with her indulgent father, who referred to her as 'Miss Hussey'. Her husband, twelve years older than she, was a handsome, easy-going man, fond of the ladies and of cards. Financed by Lord Delaval Lord Tyrconnel had bought Claremont, Surrey, in 1787. The estate had been developed by Vanbrugh for himself, and his house was later replaced by a mansion designed by Capability Brown and Henry Holland. It was another delightful place for the Delavals to meet and enjoy themselves, and make improvements to the house with the help of Robert and James Adam.

Some weeks after the performance of the *Fair Penitent* Henry Swinburne wrote to a friend that Lord Strathmore was now part of the family at Seaton Delaval and Swinburne had been invited to see a performance of *Othello*. The Moor was played by Lord Tyrconnel, Desdemona by Lady Tyrconnel, Iago by Lord Delaval, and Cassio by Lord Strathmore. Swinburne found it very indifferently acted by all except Lord Delaval. There were frequent exchanges between Lord Strathmore and the energetic, pleasure-loving family at Seaton Delaval, and his friendship with Lady Tyrconnel grew.

Meanwhile at Gibside Lord Strathmore undertook the day-to-day maintenance of the estate. The Gibside Cash Accounts were restarted in January 1791, and although they were not kept with the meticulous detail of George Bowes' time, they give a guide to the repairs and improvements undertaken in the first years of Lord Strathmore's ownership, and of new building on the estate. A bill dated 1790 showed that Lord Strathmore was trying to replace some of the trees felled by his stepfather Stoney Bowes:

> Tree Bill Account The Hon. Lord Strathmore to Archd. Dickson & Son 1790 for Gibside

| | | |
|---|---|---|
| Jany. 2nd | 1000 Oaks 3 ft. | 3. 0. 0 |
| 11 | 16500 two year Seedling Oaks | 8. 5. 0 |
| 23 | 5000 Seedling Elms | 1. 15. 4 |
| Mar. 7 | 200 Crab stock | 0. 5. 0 |
| | 200 Mapell stock | 0. 15. 0 |
| | 3 dwf peaches Two year trained | 0. 15. 0 |
| | 1 do one year trained | 0. 3. 6 |

He cared for the history of Gibside, and saw to it that the model made for George Bowes' statue of Liberty was repaired:

> By House Expenses. Paid Richard Farington repairing and Gilding the Model of the Figure of Liberty £1 15s.[2]

In 1791 window shutters were put up in the Green House built by his mother, hot house frames were repaired, the interior of the Banqueting House white-washed and oakum used to repair the Bath. Repairs were also made to Gibside House, and the Octagon Basin cleaned out. Thomas Yellowly, plumber, worked on various buildings, and also the Chapel during August 1791.

## *Innovations at Gibside*

New buildings erected by Lord Strathmore were at first small additions to the estate and its nearby farms. His grandfather, the 8th Earl, had enclosed land near Glamis Castle and made remarkable parks and plantations. This enclosure was continued by the 9th Earl, who lowered the level of Forfar Loch in 1770, gaining rich deposits of marl to fertilise the soil. He also built new farmhouses and planted a great number of trees. The 10th Earl followed the example set at Glamis by improving Cut Thorn farm at Gibside. It became the home farm of the estate, and four buildings were added to it by the new owner. A barn was built at Cut Thorn and at the end of November 1791 Thomas Thompson measured and valued it. A year later Richard Maugham & Partners were paid for 'putting on the Roof of the Hemble at Cutthorns' and in the following January they were 'making Stalls for cattle at Cutthorns Fold'. The farm was situated on the old approach to Gibside House and some care was taken to make the new buildings attractive. The Fold was to the south of the farm buildings, situated near the cart or carriage way to the farm. The random rubble wall facing the carriage way was coursed, but that away from the drive was not, an economy which would not have been countenanced in George Bowes' time. A wooden door led into the Fold, which was approximately 40 feet wide and 30 feet long. The building was U-shaped with a U-shaped space at its centre. The centre space was made up of three arches which supported a sloping roof which was almost apsidal. By this device the supporting beams had a reasonably small span. Stalls were symmetrically placed, four on each side of the central door, in a Palladian manner, and lined on the inside with rosy red brick. The Fold yard was situated to the south of the building below the level of Hill Head Lane. The wall of the yard acted as a buttress to the Lane above. The yard gave shelter to the stock, with access by gates on each side.

Stables were built at Cut Thorn in March 1803 and a Cow House in the following September. This was another building erected on principles following the enlightened agricultural movement of the time, which gave consideration to the needs of animals. A feeding passage ran the length of the building with a series of doors opening from it on one side, through which to feed each cow. At the front of the building were three doors with tethering rings nearby. Here horses were tethered while hay and fodder were unloaded. The building is still serviceable today.

In October 1793 Richard Maugham & Partners were 'taking Down the old Houses at the Coach Way Gate' in an effort to improve the entry to Gibside. A new hot house was built in the following year, and glazed at the cost of £42. The lighting of fires to air the Bath and Banqueting Houses was resumed, and a new lodge built at the gates to Warren Haugh, the south west entry to the estate, in 1795.

Lord Strathmore bought Claremont Lodge, Surrey about a mile from Lord Tyrconnel's seat at Claremont, in the summer of 1792. His friendship with Lady Tyrconnel grew, but was prevented from taking a more serious turn by her father. Lord Delaval kept drafts of his correspondence, and noted in 1795:

> Wrote to Hussey from Doncaster
> Wrote in strong terms that the Engagement could not take place. That both the Gentleman and the Lady would overturn their happy prospects which they had of comfort if she acted discreetly, and be involved in inextricable difficulties if they entered this year into any Engagement – and that therefore it cannot be – May 13 – 1795.[3]

The couple had wished to regularise their attachment, in spite of her marriage to Tyrconnel, but had been forbidden to do so by her father.

Lord Strathmore shared a love of horses with Lady Tyrconnel, who exercised the horses at Gibside. He maintained the Streatlam stud, and kept racing horses at Esher, Surrey. He also had his mother's love of growing things, and took care that buildings such as the Green House were kept in good repair. Slates were replaced on its roof in 1796, and the steps before it altered. In December the same year a new Peach House was begun, and Hugh Hopes paid for 'building a Wall making Flues, Chimney &c. in Garden Wall for Ditto'. Peach House frames were added, and vinery slides made.

In January 1798 a new lodge was first mentioned in the Cash Accounts, and by April 'new lodges' were referred to. Lord Strathmore was building double lodges at the edge of Snipes Dene Wood, where the New Coach Way entered the Hollinside estate. They were situated to the north east of Gibside House, and about 20 yards before the Coach Way entered Hollinside Park. They were plain rectangular buildings approximately 18 x 12 feet in size, with pyramidal slate roofs. These lodges no longer exist, but were shown on the Whickham Tithe Map of 1842, made from several surveys by Thomas Bell. Martha Helen Davidson showed them in her 'Gibside Sketch Book' of 1827. They were similar to the estate lodges which now form the entrance to Whickham Golf Course, but the latter were castellated, and built after 1856. There was still trouble with vandals at Gibside, and they may have been built as a deterrent, as well as keeping pace with fashion. They took nearly two years to build, and were in use by August 1800.

Lord Strathmore became involved with the Gibside Volunteers at the end of 1797. He wished to raise a company of cavalry under his command to withstand attack by Napoleon. This entailed the raising and training of troops, in much the same way as George Bowes had done at the time of the 1745 rebellion. Like his grandfather he had served in the army and became the leader of the local volunteer force when need arose.

34. Gibside House, engraving after William Norris.

Lady Tyrconnel became a more constant visitor to Gibside, and assured her father, Lord Delaval, 'I continue to keep very good hours, & take proper riding & walking exercise'. She was suffering from consumption, and her condition varied. She complained to her father 'I have been so poorly' and 'my sickness plagues me again'. In September 1800 Dr. George Ocheltrie wrote to Lord Delaval that he had 'just arrive from Gibside' where he had been for two days:

> I left her Ladyship in good spirits, & she finds herself a great deal better since she went there, the winds being so variable, had an impressive effect upon her Ladyship, so near the sea as Seaton Delaval and I trust in God the change of air will answer the desired purpose.[4]

Remedies were useless and Lady Tyrconnel died at Gibside on 8 October 1800.

Like George Bowes on the death of his first wife, Eleanor Verney, his grandson found consolation and employment in the estate at Gibside. He was now an unattached bachelor of over 30 with a large sprawling mansion at Gibside, and a further property to the south at Streatlam Castle. His enthusiasm in architecture was for the Gothick mode, not the delicate rococo-Gothick used by his grandfather for the Banqueting House in the early 1740s, but the more robust Gothick especially popular in Northumberland. The Duke of Northumberland had popularized the style, which was taken up by Lord Delaval at Ford Castle, and many other landowners in the county.

Little save routine repairs had been made at Gibside House by Lord Strathmore. Some rooms were added, one 'behind the house' in 1794, which may have been in the servants' quarters. The first improvement was not structural, and can be deduced from details shown on John Dobson's 'Plans of Gibside House showing the proposed addition' designed some years later in 1814. The north elevation in this composite plan shows that the five original central bays had octagonal glazing bars by the time Dobson made his design. The windows are shown in black, and additions in red. A double octagon is shown in each of these sashes, while the others have six lights to each sash. A lower sash containing the octagonal glazing bars still remains in place in one of the first floor windows. The opening had been blocked up for a staircase to be made in the house, and the glazing bars were thus protected. That these windows existed in this form, was confirmed during a survey of the ruined house made by Ian Curry in 1986 when two oak window sashes with a double octagon pattern were found. This tallies with an entry in the

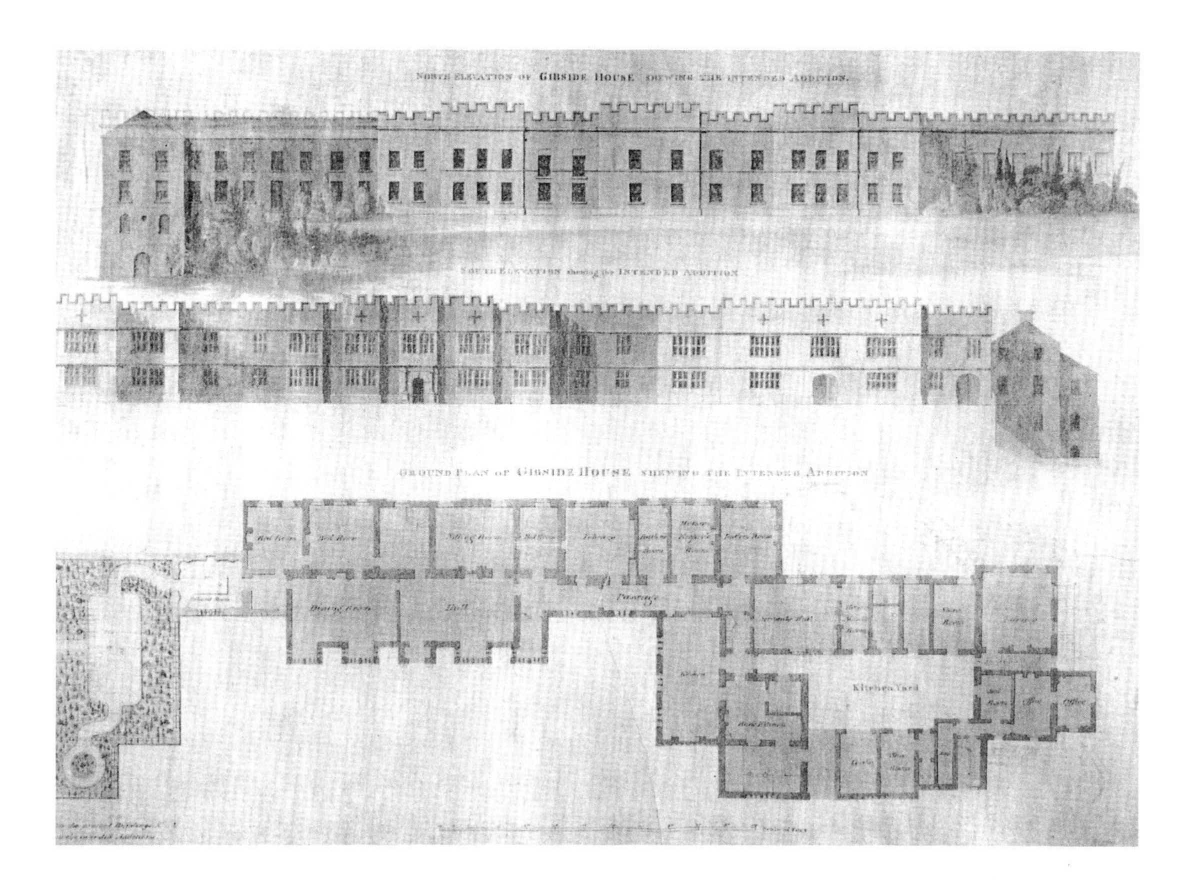

35. North and South elevations of Gibside House, and Plan, by John Dobson, 1814.

Gibside Cash Accounts for 24 March 1801:

> By Lord Strathmore Paid Mr. Lamb for the Northumberland Glass... for Crown & Flint as P [er] particulars. £126 1s 11d

Hexagonal panes of glass had been used in the Banqueting House in 1742 and it is not easy to discover when the octagonal panes were introduced into the north-facing windows of Gibside House. If the entry for Northumberland glass refers to the octagon panes it seems likely that Lord Strathmore was indulging his taste for the romantic and the Gothick mode.

Accounts vary as to how far Gibside House was rebuilt in the first years of the nineteenth century. The date 1805 given above the reconstructed porch may have been the date when Lord Strathmore took up residence at Gibside once more, but the record of building started in summer 1803 and work was still in progress in 1812. In a letter about the survey Ian Curry ruled out the suggestion that the 17th century house was totally demolished in 1805. He thought that the theory given in the second edition of Pevsner's *County Durham* (1983) was plausible and 'that Gilkie added the present heavy parapet in place of the third story of the earlier house'. He also thought that the mullioned bays of the south front must be original as:

> it seems unlikely that, if they had been demolished, Gilkie would have rebuilt them in that form – his heavy parapet needed something rather more substantial to

36. Gibside Chapel, after Sopwith.

support it and I expect he would have taken the opportunity to provide this had it arisen. Alexander Gilkie (*c.* 1756-1834) is not mentioned in the House-Building Accounts until the 18 January 1808, when he was paid 13 guineas.[5]

Gilkie, a master-builder of Coldstream, had been recommended to Strathmore by Lord Delaval who had employed him for some of the alterations and additions to Ford Castle.[6] There Lord Delaval had built a tall battlemented parapet with cross-loops to part of the south elevation of the Castle, and a similar giant parapet was erected at Gibside in place of the dismantled third storey. Gilkie was responsible for towers and a theatrical entrance gate at Ford Castle described in his specification made for Lord Delaval in 1801. He must have seen how Ford Castle had been re-embattled, and used a similar construction at Gibside with a high parapet to conceal the pitched roof. He appears to have given a plan only for the alteration, and no further payment was made to him. William Bell of Newcastle, who was paid £100 on 18 January 1810, must have supervised the alteration work.

William Bell (active 1786-1810) is a little-known figure. He was one of the five architects who submitted plans in 1786 for the rebuilding of All Saints' Church, Newcastle. There is no documentary evidence of the plans submitted by Mr. Bell, but a William Bell was listed as one of the four church wardens at All Saints' in 1800. William Bell, joiner, near Stockbridge, is listed in *The Newcastle and Gateshead Directory* for 1795, and this address links him with William Bell who worked at St. Cuthbert's College, Ushaw, County Durham. The address Stockbridge, which was near to All Saints' Church, is given on one of his bills at Ushaw for 1805. It appears that he acted as job architect for plans made by James Taylor of Islington for the building of the College from 1804-9. In one of the bills for Ushaw he is described as 'surveyor'. His work at Gibside also appears to have been supervising the plans made by others. From 1803 to January 1810 £9,655 11s 4 ½d had been paid for the work at Gibside House.

Apart from making the main part of the house more compact by removing the top storey of the house, Lord Strathmore altered the kitchen offices, which had never proved satisfactory in the 18th century. The two amorphous wings which contained extensions to the house and kitchen, and were shown on the map of 1767 were regularised into a kitchen court. These alterations were complete by 1803 and were shown on the plan of the estate made by John Fryer in that year. John Dobson's plan showing proposed additions of 1814 indicated what had been achieved. The rest of the ground floor retained its now old-fashioned arrangement of rooms with three north-facing bedrooms leading directly into the entrance hall and dining room, with no corridor. In most fashionable houses bedrooms were by now located on the first floor. A passage led from the older part of the house past the library to the butler's pantry. A small staircase with a skew entrance was situated between the library and butler's pantry, with easy access to the cellar for both the owner and butler. The house-keeper's room was situated opposite the kitchen and the offices were well-planned, apart from the fact that the dining room and kitchen were at opposite ends of the house. The servants' hall faced north and was near both the kitchen and back kitchen. A large laundry was situated over the brew house, and the kitchen yard divided the servants' day quarters from the coal house, shoe room and the room with an engine for raising water. There was a safe for plate and valuables, with a bedroom nearby so watch might constantly be kept by a servant. Here too were offices to deal with the tenantry and estate matters. The servants could now comfortably be accommodated in their own quarters, and not kept on hand to do messages, as they could now easily be summoned by bell rope. Bell systems had begun to be installed in the 1760s and '70s, and in May 1798 fashionable bell ropes with chintz tassels were installed at Gibside House.[7]

37. Gibside Chapel, Interior of Dome.

The Earl of Strathmore lived in considerable style, as a list of his male servants, horses, mules and dogs shows. The list covered from 5 April 1798 to the same date in 1799 and must have been for tax purposes. It shows that at Gibside he kept: agent, gardener, game-keeper, four grooms, footman, valet and coachman. At Streatlam he had: stud groom, groom, stable boy, gamekeeper and gardener. At Gibside he had 2 four-wheeled carriages, 14 horses for riding, 16 for other purposes and 14 farm horses with 7 dogs. The list shows that although Streatlam housed his stud, most of the horses were at Gibside.

During this time Lord Strathmore did not neglect his family. In 1802 the gardens at Bird Hill House to the east of Gibside, were included in the husbandry of the estate. Later his sister Anna Maria Jessup and her two daughters came to live there. He kept up his friendship with the family at Seaton Delaval and for a while turned his attention to Lady Tyrconnel's daughter, Lady Susan Carpenter. It was over ten years since he had been 'desperately smitten' by her mother, and when he finally proposed to Lady Susan she refused him because of his coldness and lack of concern for her.

## *The completion of the Chapel*

George Bowes' hopes for a Chapel to adorn his estate and house the bodies of his successors had

38. Gibside Chapel, Pulpit and Pews.

not yet been fully realised. The Chapel had been made weather-tight and the decoration of the interior continued up to the cornice when Mary Eleanor discontinued the building of the Chapel in 1769. The elaborate coffering of the dome and ceiling alcoves shown in James Paine's section of the Chapel was not carried out. Instead the ribs of the ceiling vaults were decorated with stucco, which also outlined the ceiling panels. The centre of the dome was filled by a mundane flower motif, and the panels above the niches, left plain in Paine's section, were decorated with crudely designed palm branches.

According to records in the account book 'Buildings at Gibside House' work was renewed in January 1811 when William Smith was paid for joiner work at Gibside Chapel. Ralph Watson, mason, and William Smith undertook most of the decoration of the Chapel before its consecration in 1812. Joseph Robson began the plasterwork in 1811, and by 1816 had been paid £583 9s 6d for his labours. At the same time Thomas Hall was paid £439 10s 2d for mason work.[8]

The main furnishings of the Chapel were of cherry-wood in an elegant style of the beginning of the 19th century. The three-decker pulpit was used according to the importance of the teaching given, with a clerk's desk, reading desk and the topmost level for preaching. The pulpit was surmounted by an oval sounding board supported by an Ionic column. There were box pews with curved seats in the two side apses, and square box pews for the family and other important members of the congregation near the door. Work on the Chapel House for the resident

39. Gibside House, Kitchen Wing.

Chaplain began in 1813 and it was completed the following year.

In 1809 Lord Strathmore formed the longest-lasting attachment of his life. He met the beautiful Mary Millner when she was 22 years old, and working at Wemmergill Hall, his estate in Lunedale, part of the Pennines to the west of Streatlam. Her parents came from Stainton a mile from Streatlam Castle. A son was born to them in London on 19 June 1811, and was christened John after his father. The couple remained in London with their son for about a year, and then Mary and her child went to live at Wemmergill Hall. After a further twelve months they moved to Streatlam Castle, where Mary lived as Lord Strathmore's wife. She was however uneasy in company, and did not act as hostess when guests were present.

Lord Strathmore now had a wife in all but name, and a small son to whom he was devoted. However, as long as they remained at Streatlam Mary Millner would never be more than his mistress to the villagers and servants at the Castle, and it may have been this fact that caused him to ask John Dobson (1787-1865) to make plans for additions to Gibside House. If she were to move there as his wife they would be starting afresh, and without the prejudice they found at Streatlam. Dobson's beautiful presentation drawing of the plan for Gibside and its intended additions, together with the north and south elevations on the same sheet, show his skill as a draughtsman. In 1814 when the drawing was made Dobson was still building up his practice, which was to become the most successful in the north east. He would have had time to make such

40. Section of proposed Orangery for Gibside House, by Dobson, 1814.

drawings himself, as well as the sketches on which they were based. Dobson's plan added a billiard room and conservatory to the west end of the house. The billiard room, as well as being fashionable, would have separated the rest of the house from any unpleasant smells of earth and damp, as recommended by Humphry Repton (1752-1818). The conservatory was to be two storeys high and to match the battlemented parapets with cross-loops of the rest of the house. It also balanced the recently reconstructed kitchen wing. Further battlements were also to be added to the north face of the kitchen wing to make the roof finish uniform. The longitudinal section of the projected conservatory shows slender cast iron columns with fretted Gothic arches supporting a hipped roof of glass panels. Cast iron, which had been used for columns to support galleries in theatres and churches, was also used in the building of mills to reduce the risk of fire. The use of cast iron for architectural purposes seems to have come through horticulture. John Nash (1752-1835) was an early exponent:

> In 1798, John Nash exhibited at the Royal Academy a "Conservatory for His Royal Highness the Price of Wales". The drawing, preserved at Windsor, shows a simple three-aisle structure with slim columns, presumably of iron, and iron roof-trusses consisting of a series of diminishing rings between rafters and the tie-beam. The design was almost certainly not executed...[9]

Dobson's conservatory was also a three-aisle

41. Gibside from the South, by J.M.W. Turner, watercolour, *c.* 1817.

structure but four main internal columns were arranged to support the hipped roof only and did not continue up to the ends of the building. A further variation in shape which made it differ from Nash's simple shed-like building, was the addition of the domed area to the south. Dobson was a skilful engineer in cast iron, and this must have been one of his earliest plans using the material.

Matching windows facing the kitchen wing were shown on the interior wall of the conservatory. An elaborate heating system was housed at the back of the building and underfloor heating reached two of the pillars shown in Dobson's section. Nothing came of the plan and Lord Strathmore and Mary Millner continued to live at Streatlam as before.

On 7 August 1815 a further honour was added to his Scottish title when the 10th Earl of Strathmore was created a peer of the United Kingdom by the style and title of Baron Bowes of Streatlam in the County of Durham and of Lunedale in the County of York. Gibside was not mentioned in the citation, which referred to Streatlam, the Bowes' family seat, and Lunedale where he met Mary Millner. In November 1817 Turner (1775-1851) visited Gibside to make drawings and sketches for Robert Surtees' *History of Durham.* He made two watercolour views of Gibside, a romantic view from the north and one from the south that was both romantic and accurate in the delineation of the landscape and its buildings. Unfortunately these pictures, now in the Bowes' Museum, Barnard Castle, are on a small scale which makes recognition of buildings on the estate difficult.

The marriage of Lord Strathmore and Mary Millner finally took place at St. George's, Hanover Square, London on 2 July 1820. He was ill, but was able to make the responses at the ceremony, and declared it was one of the happiest moments of his life. The next day he made a last codicil to his will making it clear that his bequests to Mary Millner would now be hers as Countess of Strathmore, and shortly afterwards died. On his father's death his son John ceased to be Lord Glamis and his guardians claimed the title of Earl of Strathmore for him. However, there was another claimant, his uncle the Honourable Thomas Bowes claimed the title Earl of Strathmore, and laid claim to his brother's property in Scotland. His claim was upheld by the courts, and the nine-year old John Bowes inherited only his father's English property. After the death of the 10th Earl of Strathmore George Bowes' direct descendants were never to use Gibside as their family home.

CHAPTER

9

# JOHN BOWES 1811-1885

# *The Absentee Landlord*

With the death of the 10th Earl of Strathmore the great days of Gibside had passed. The estate no longer had an owner willing to spend regular sums on its upkeep and improvement, or who wished to live there permanently. His son was already at boarding school and later went to Eton. The estate was run by his mother and the trustees of his father's will. By the age of nineteen the young John Bowes was taking an active interest in the trustees' management of his estate. Bowes' education was completed at Trinity College, Cambridge, where his tutor was William Hutt. Before he left the university in 1831 Hutt had become his step-father. As a young man embarking on his career Bowes had no wish to live at Gibside, and was delighted when the Countess of Strathmore and her husband decided to use Gibside House as their country residence.

Bowes became a member of Parliament in 1832 and when visiting the north he did not often live at Streatlam, but stayed with his mother and Hutt at Gibside. He had great respect for Hutt, who in his absence would look after Gibside and colliery matters with the help of Ralph Dent, the agent for the combined estates of Streatlam and Gibside. After 1846 Bowes lived for a long time mainly in France. Estate business, both at Streatlam and Gibside, was dealt with during short summer visits.

The year 1852 was a memorable one for Bowes. He was made High Sheriff for the County of Durham and travelled from France to perform some of his duties. His horse, Daniel O'Rourke, brought him his third Derby win, and a new collier, the 'John Bowes', the first steam collier to be built at Palmer's yard at Jarrow, was launched on the Tyne. Bowes married Joséphine Coffin-Chevallier at a civil ceremony in Paris on 23 August 1852, and called at the recently purchased Château at Louveciennes before going on honeymoon. His luck held in 1853 when he won the Derby with 'West Australian'.

His situation was now more settled and he was finally able to dispose of the theatre in Paris which he had bought for Joséphine. In 1851 when £5,000 was needed to drain land at Gibside, authority had been asked to charge this sum on the estate. Now Bowes found that his financial situation was better and some money could be spent on improving the buildings at Gibside. He sent instructions concerning the upkeep of Gibside during William Hutt's occupation in 1854. The Bath House, which was beginning to decay in 1827 when sketched by Martha Helen Davidson, had been engulfed by a landslip and Bowes wrote to his agent at Gibside, William Thompson:

> The Bath walk is I am afraid a bad affair, of course Mr. Hutt cannot be expected to go to the expence of restoring it to the estate it was in some time since & I do not think there is any object in my doing so. Perhaps the best thing would be to confine what is done to prevent further slips.[1]

He also directed that a small building to the west of Gibside House, the Necessary House erected by George Bowes, was to be carefully taken down and the stones used in the future, perhaps for an entrance lodge. Mr. Hutt proposed to put someone to live in the kitchen of the Banqueting House to prevent vandalism, but Bowes thought the room would be too small to live in.[2] At the same time a specification was made for joinery and carpentry work in renewing 'the roof, doors and windows of the houses in the gardens at Gibside'.

The following year Bowes turned his attention to the Green House, and in March 1855 wrote in his memorandum book:

> The Greenhouse at Gibside has now been completely altered & converted to a Conservatory at a cost of £736. 10. 3. An Orchid House is to be put up in the Garden. The road across Warren Haugh, & in the Green Close to be opened out, & Altered according to my direction.[3]

This changed the character of the Green

EUG. FEYEN.
1863.

House and the hipped slate roof was converted to six small pitches of glass with a line of iron support columns across the building. These were hollow and acted as drainage pipes from the roof. The height of the two small entry lobbies was reduced and today the holes for the joists of the new roof can be seen breaking into the relieving arches over the doors. The rounded corners of the lobbies were altered and the whole plastered and rendered. A large stage or planter was built in the centre of the Green House using 18th century bricks with two dressed sandstone string courses and a stone coping. Low walls surrounded the stage and were also of brick. In the ruined condition of the Green House today it is difficult to make out what the alterations were, but the remains of the grill of the 19th century heating system and stone edging for the Victorian planting beds still remain.[4]

A more imposing entrance to the Gibside estate was made some time after 1856 and perhaps stones from the ruined Necessary House were used for building a lodge as Bowes had suggested.[5] Castellated double lodges were built at the entry on Fellside Road and the lengthened drive curved through the Hollinside estate to reach Gibside. Mary, Countess of Strathmore, died in 1860, and although William Hutt was granted another lease for 21 years, it is likely that the lodges were built in Mary's lifetime.

Following Hutt's advice Bowes drastically thinned the trees at Gibside in 1859 and 1860. In all probability these were the ones planted by his father in 1790 to replace those cut down by Stoney Bowes. Hutt thought that the trees would be worth £8,000 to £10,000 and this meant that the estate showed a profit for these years. Hutt remarried within a year of the Countess of Strathmore's death. Bowes was hurt and disquieted by this action, as he thought it showed disrespect for his mother's memory, but he was finally reconciled.

42. Portrait of John Bowes, by Eugene Feyen, 1863.

In June 1863 William Thompson reported on the condition of the Banqueting House. Some repairs had already been carried out:

> The lead roof was taken off during the year 1862 and replaced with a new one of corrugated iron, which is in good order there are new conductors and downcoming pipes as well as the the outside walls & parapets are in very good condition.[6]

He reported that the floor of the Ante-Room needed repair and the window of the adjoining closet was in a bad state, but that the plasterwork on the walls and ceiling was in good condition. He described the floor of the Great Room as 'a good specimen of workmanship of the day when it was made'. The woodwork needed painting and the plasterwork was in a very good state of preservation though a little stained in one or two places on the ceiling. The walls and ceiling of the kitchen were covered in plasterwork at this time, which was in good repair, and the stairs leading from it to the roof were in a good state.

In November 1869 John Bowes noted:

> Parts of the offices, &c at the Hall at Gibside having been found to be in a dangerous state – they have been taken down, the defective foundations remedied, & are now in the course of being rebuilt, & completed[7]

Hutt was knighted in 1865 and some years later, in 1874, he gave up the lease of Gibside and retired to his estate on the Isle of Wight. Gibside House was let to Mr. Robert Lamb of Axwell Park at an increased rent.

The estate had always needed constant maintenance, and in December 1875 J. E. Watson (1821-1885), the Newcastle architect, examined Gibside Chapel. The Chapel roof was repaired the following year with new timber and lead. John Bowes wrote in his memorandum book in December 1875:

> Damage to houses & buildings by pitworkings to be settled for – care to be taken that the coal is not worked near the stables & Monument.

This is a situation which has continued to the present day. The coal which had been the origin of George Bowes' wealth, was also to cause the destruction by settlement of some of his carefully planned buildings.

John Bowes' interests were elsewhere. After his marriage he continued to live in France, and he and his wife made the Château at Louveciennes their home. Towards the end of the 1850s they began to collect pictures and other material for a museum, keeping their collection in a temporary gallery they built in Paris. They visited Streatlam each year, and according to Augustus Hare, a distant relative, made a very full programme for visitors, with every moment occupied. They decided that their museum should be situated at Barnard Castle three miles from Streatlam. At the end of their visit to Streatlam Castle in 1864 Bowes asked his solicitor to buy some fields on the outskirts of the town and by the following year they had most of the land they wanted for the museum. Jules Pellechet (1829-1903), whose father had worked for Bowes, designed the museum, and his plans were interpreted by the local architect J. E. Watson. The foundation stone of the Bowes Museum was laid in 1869, and when completed in 1875 it afforded the unlikely spectacle of a French château built near Barnard Castle, a thriving market town on the banks of the River Tees.

John Bowes died in 1885. His assets fell short of his bequests, and through lack of a direct heir his estates in England reverted to the Earl of Strathmore and the Bowes Lyon family.

CHAPTER

# 10

# *The Legacy of George Bowes*

George Bowes' intention that Gibside was to be a family home for his descendants and that they should follow his example in its upkeep, was not fulfilled. What he did achieve was the creation of a landscape that would endure even if neglected. He created pleasure grounds at Gibside from lands which up to that time had produced some iron, and timber particularly useful for making charcoal. The grounds had also been extensively mined for coal with little thought of the desolation this might cause. Gibside House was reported to stand on a pillar of coal while mining had taken place around it. At the time the plantations were being made and the estate laid out, Bowes did not lose sight of the fact that growing timber was profitable, and would help finance the estate in future. The price to be paid was bare areas while trees were growing, and these he made more interesting with garden buildings.

Bowes was a practical man and while the buildings he erected at Gibside enhanced his grounds they were not usually merely ornamental. His one great gesture of self-aggrandisement however, the tall Column to Liberty with its gilded statue, was visible to a large part of the Derwent Valley.

Bowes was not an originator. He studied some of the influential architecture books of the day, and with the help of Sir Thomas Robinson equipped himself to become a discerning judge of architecture. His only recorded visit to an estate famed for its landscaped grounds was to Stowe. Lord Perceval wrote of his impressions of Stowe in 1724, that it:

> has gained the reputation of being the finest seat in England... The Gardens, by reason of good contrivance of the walks, seem to be three times as large as they are. They contain but 28 acres yet it took us up to two hours.[1]

The estate at Gibside including the Hollinside purchase of 1735, consisted of just over 1,000 acres in all. It did not have the numerous temples, summerhouses and statues which made a tour of the gardens at Stowe both long and memorable, but a small number of buildings strategically placed so that visitors would explore the nineteen walks. Farmland was part of the landscape to be enjoyed, with a fosse to keep cattle away when necessary. The pleasure grounds merged with the fields, while the stone for some of Bowes' buildings was quarried on the estate.

Of Bowes' neighbours in County Durham only John Burdon at Hardwick, near Sedgefield, could compare with Bowes in the layout of his estate. Burdon had the advantage of having James Paine to design all the garden buildings at Hardwick, and they were built in the short space of three years from 1754-7. The site however was flat and did not have the varied terrain which made Gibside so attractive. The layout at Hardwick was not a life time's work as the planning and execution of the buildings at Gibside, and Burdon was eventually bankrupted by the expense of his estate.

Visitors such as Bishop Pococke had admired Gibside and the Swedish traveller Angerstein described its 'splendid park and magnificent buildings'. Another visitor was the spritely blue stocking, Mrs. Montagu, of Denton Hall, Newcastle. She wrote to the naturalist Benjamin Stillingfleet in October 1758, comparing Gibside with Lowther, Westmorland, and found the trees at Lowther overpowering. Bowes was proud of his property and the grounds were open to visitors at certain times.

Artists drew and painted Gibside for it was a time when travel books and topographical works were popular. Edward Dayes (1763-1854) painted 'A view of Gibside Park from Goodshields Haugh', probably in the early 1790s. The watercolour shows picturesque trees on one side with rolling countryside, banked trees in the distance and the Column to Liberty. It is now owned by the National Gallery of Scotland. J.M.W. Turner toured the British Isles for subjects to illustrate in his sketchbooks and for publication. Turner wrote to his friend and watercolourist, James Holworthy, on 21st November 1817 'Lord Strathmore called at

43. Aerial view of Gibside.

Raby and took me away to the North'. His two small watercolours of Gibside are delicate and colourful and he also painted another of Lord Strathmore's properties, Hylton Castle, near Sunderland. These painters must have had some influence when their works were published in making Gibside better known, but its secluded situation, Bowes' 'retired place', meant that it did not have the influence of the buildings put up in his parks by the Duke of Northumberland. The Duke as well as being the wealthiest man in Northumberland, had his country estate at Alnwick on the Great North Road and accessible to those of the Northumberland gentry who wished to see his improvements and follow his example.

Of all the admirers of Gibside, James Paine, in his *Plans, Elevations and Sections of Noblemen and Gentlemen's Houses* (1767) made the most fitting judgement of George Bowes and and his estate, when describing the Chapel:

> Gibside is remarkable as one of the finest places in the north of *England*, for woods, fine walks, garden-buildings, &c. this building is erected at the end of a most beautiful terras, which commands extensive views of the adjacent country, and of the valley through which the Derwent runs, the other is terminated by woods and the largest column in *England*, except the monument in *London*. The whole of these gardens, buildings &c. were the production of the very worthy owner.[2]

Paine wrote that George Bowes was responsible for the gardens and the buildings at Gibside.

This was courtesy and not literally true, but Bowes had been the mainspring of the concept, and had seen that his ideas were carried through. His plan when building was to use the best possible materials and workmanship, and he built to last.

Today, over 200 years after his death, a surprising number of his buildings at Gibside survive in spite of bad treatment. The paths and rides he made through the trees have largely been respected by the Forestry Commission, which until recently ran the woodlands. The Octagon Basin, though overgrown, provides visitors to the Banqueting House with a view of water, one of the elements in landscape advocated by Switzer. The Banqueting House itself, sadly ruined until 1979, was saved by the Landmark Trust and skilfully restored by Ian Curry. Since the restoration was completed in 1980 many visitors there have delighted in the landscape created by George Bowes. Some years ago the Stables were used as a farm, but later were deserted. It is hoped that they may be restored to their original state. The Ice House, once hidden by undergrowth, has a newly constructed path past its door. The walled garden retains its rosy red brick walls, but the flued walls to ripen fruit are disused. George Bowes' most conspicuous structure, the Column to Liberty, stands with its figure gazing towards Gibside House.

The Green House, his daughter's contribution to the buildings at Gibside, lies in ruins. Altered to a Victorian conservatory by her grandson and a prey to present-day vandals, the columns of its arcade are still impressive. Various suggestions have been made for its use, but so far without results.

The most striking building on the estate, the Chapel, begun the year Bowes died, stands serene at the end of the Great Walk. Bowes' Mausoleum and the Chapel above was given to the National Trust by the 16th Earl of Strathmore in 1965. The gift included the avenue and restrictive covenants over adjoining land were also granted. In April 1993 the Trust bought the freehold of Gibside Estate from the 18th Earl of Strathmore, and hope by careful stewardship to restore the pleasure grounds to much of their former glory. Meanwhile the Palladian beauty of the Chapel enhances the grand, long-enduring idyll, created by George Bowes.

## ABBREVIATIONS AND MSS. USED IN THE NOTES

BL British Library, London (Bowes and Egmont Papers)
DBL Darlington Branch Library, Crown Street, Local History Section (Bowes Papers)
DRO Durham Record Office (Strathmore Estate Archives, The Right Hon. The Earl of Strathmore and Kinghorne)
GPL Gateshead Public Library, Local History Section (Cotesworth Papers)
Glamis Glamis Castle, Strathmore Estates (Bowes Papers)
HMC Historic Manuscripts Commission (Earl of Carlisle Papers)
LCRO Lancashire County Record Office
NLS National Library of Scotland, Edinburgh (MS 1080. Anonymous Journal writer of 1789)
NCRO Northumberland County Record Office (Delaval Papers)
TWAD Tyne and Wear Archives Department, Blandford House (Newcastle Infirmary Minute Books)

## NOTES

In the text, before the adoption of the Gregorian Calendar in England in 1752, the year is taken to begin with 1 January and not 25 March, and the dates of documentary references changed accordingly.

In quoting direct from a MS, the original spelling and punctuation are kept, save raised letters are lowered and archaic forms such as ye (the) and yt (that) are modernised.

### Chapter 1: The Bowes Brothers

1 – Hughes, *North Country Life* p 17
2 – Glamis, Bowes MSS Vol. 24 p 71
3 – BL Add. MS 40747, Bowes MSS II f 142
4 – Ibid., fs 160-1
5 – Ibid., f 165
6 – Ibid., f 164. The South Sea Company was founded in 1711 to trade with Spanish South America, a trade which was to deal largely in slaves. The government hoped that its profits would help to reduce the National Debt and at first the shares sold well. After the Treaty of Utrecht ending war with Spain in 1713, trade, including that in slaves, was curtailed by Spanish taxes and prospects for the Company were not good. In February 1718 King George I became Governor of the South Sea Company and the outlook for the Company looked more favourable. However the King neither attended meetings of the Court of Directors nor the General Court of Proprietors and the Company was without strong leadership.
William Bowes' letter to his mother was dated 20th March 1718 and presumably South Sea stock was falling in the month following the change of the Governor of the Company. The crash of the Company, or the South Sea Bubble, did not take place until two years later in Autumn 1720, when many subscribers were ruined.
7 – Surtees, *History of Durham*, Vol. IV p102
8 – BL Add. MS 40747 Bowes MSS II fs 174
9 – Ibid., fs 176-7
10 – Ibid., f 182
11 – Ibid., f 184

### Chapter 2: The Count

1 – Glamis, Bowes MSS Vol. 26 letter 48
2 – I am grateful to Dr. Eric Clavering for background to the Clavering family.
3 – Halsband, *Letters Lady Mary Wortley Montagu* Vol. II p 91
4 – HMC *Carlisle* p 106
5 – DRO D/St/V988 Cash Accounts 12 October 1739
6 – DRO D/St/V991 Cash Accounts 24 June 1752

7 – Wills, 'One of its kind. The Newcastle Infirmary', *Country Life* 185 (10 October 1991) p 124
8 – DRO D/St/ Box 355
9 – DRO D/St/V944 Journals 14 September 1745
10 – This must have been a long-standing friendship for Charles Avison was one of the three signatories of a codicil to George Bowes' will made in October 1758.
11 – Missasippy was a game similar to Bagatelle with balls going through numbered arches to make the score. It was a popular form of gaming for over a hundred years.
12 – DBL Bowes MSS Vol. XXXVI letter 20
13 – GPL Cotesworth MSS CP1/66 p 1, 21 October 1722
14 – BL Add MS 40748 Bowes MSS III f 53
15 – GPL Cotesworth MSS CP4/57 p 1
16 – Glamis, Bowes MSS Vol. 39 p 91
17 – DRO D/St/V937 Journals p 174
18 – Glamis, Bowes MSS Vol. 39 p 153
19 – Halsband, *Life of Lady Mary Wortley Montagu*, p 123
20 – GPL Cotesworth MSS CP1/237
21 – DRO D/St/V30
22 – NLS MS 1080 p 6. The height is exaggerated and today the arch is reckoned to be 80 feet above the gorge.
23 – J.M. Fewster, 'The Politics and Administration of the Borough of Morpeth' Ph D Thesis 1960 pp 53-6

## Chapter 3: This Retired Place

1 – GPL CK5/183 This map of the first Western Wagon-way of 1712, also known as the Bucksnook Way, was kindly pointed out by Dr. Eric Clavering. At the moment this map is the only documentary evidence for the village in Gibside grounds. A similar situation existed at Streatlam and the village there may have been cleared by William Blakiston Bowes in 1717-21 when he rebuilt the castle. The map of Streatlam (DRO D/St/X12) made for George Bowes in 1755 shows 'Streatlam Old Town' to the east of the castle. It is conjectured that these villagers were removed to Stainton a mile to the west of Streatlam.
2 – Glamis, Bowes MSS Vol. 8 p 28
3 – DRO D/St/V985 Cash Accounts 24 June 1731
4 – W.A. Brogden, 'Stephen Switzer and garden design', Ph D Thesis 1973 pp 1-15
5 – Ibid., p 212
6 – Angerstein, 'Resa genons England 1753-55'. From a translation kindly made available by Dr. Stafford Linsley.
7 – DRO D/St/V985 Cash Accounts 1 October 1732
8 – DRO D/St/V1202 Gibside Inventory December 1746 p 29
9 – The book 'Sketches in the Grounds at Gibside' is now in the Bowes Museum, Barnard Castle. There are 33 sketches in all with watermarks dating from 1827. The book contains drawings made of other Bowes' property including Hylton Castle, near Sunderland.
10 – Bowes was well served by his estate labourers and in spite of difficult terrain the wall still exists. It was built with holes for drainage and the blocks were secured by iron clamps. The drainage spouts are a refined version of those on Causey Arch and some of the workers may have been involved in both ventures.
11 – T. Friedman, *James Gibbs* p 121 and 318-9
12 – LCRO MS DDTO Q/10 quoted Beard, *Decorative Plasterwork* p 249
13 – DRO D/St/V943 p 158
14 – DRO D/St/Box 140 Gibside Inventory 1743
15 – DRO D/St/V986 Cash Accounts 13 July 1734
16 – *Proceedings of Newcastle Society of Antiquaries*, 2nd series, II no. 23 1886 p 186
17 – DRO D/St/V941 Journals p 228
18 – Røstvig, *The Happy Man* Vol. II p 120
19 – DRO D/St/V1203
20 – Wallington, unsigned drawing, 1735
21 – *The Newcastle Advertiser* Saturday 28 March 1789 p 2 column 4
22 – DRO D/St/V988 Cash Accounts 22 November 1739

## Chapter 4: Its Happy Situation

1 – DRO D/St/V988 Cash Accounts 19 July 1740

2 – DRO D/St/V942 Journals 6 September 1737 p 262
3 – The amphitheatre at Claremont was part of Charles Bridgeman's plan for this estate. It was situated above a small round basin which was subsequently enlarged into an irregularly shaped lake by William Kent.
4 – Colvin, *Dictionary* 2nd ed. (1978) p 332-3
5 – HMC 15th Report, Appendix VI (1897) p 194 (Carlisle Papers)
6 – Rowan, 'Gothic Restoration at Raby Castle' *Architectural History* 15 (1972) pp 25-6
7 – Leach, 'Designs for a Practical Man' *Country Life* 156 (12 August 1974) p 696
8 – TWAD, Newcastle Infirmary Minute Books, General Quarterly Court 7 July 1751
9 – DRO D/St/V988 Cash Accounts 16 November 1740
10 – DRO D/St/V942 Journals 6 September 1737
11 – Louw, 'The Sash-window' D. Phil. Thesis 1981 pp 252-4
12 – DRO D/St/V990 Cash Accounts 13 March 1746
13 – DRO D/St/V989 Cash Accounts 20 August 1742
14 – DRO D/St/V989 Cash Accounts 22 October 1743
15 - I am grateful to Miss Phoebe Lowery for the information that Philip Daniel worked at Fenham Hall.
16 – The Banqueting House was still in good condition shortly before the second World War, but by 1979 it was ruinous. The roof had fallen in, and trees and shrubs filled the space left between the rapidly decaying walls. Some stuccowork remained, but had been covered with grafitti. The Landmark Trust bought the building in 1979 and it was skilfully restored by Ian Curry of Charlewood, Curry, Wilson and Atkinson, Architects.
17 – DRO D/St/V944 Journals 24 December 1745 p 251
18 – Sykes, *Local Records* Vol. I (1865) p 181
19 – DRO D/St/V990 Cash Accounts 20 November 1747
20 – DRO D/St/V946 Journals 1748 p 161

## Chapter 5: New Beauties

1 – DRO D/St/V990 Cash Accounts 4 August 1747
2 – Ibid., 4 November 1747
3 – Pococke, 'Northern Journeys', *North Country Diaries* II, Surtees Society 124 (1914) p 239
4 – DRO D/St/Box 63
5 – DRO D/St/V1202 Gibside Inventory 1746
6 – DRO D/St/V1488 Mrs. Bowes' Cash Accounts 25 May 1748
7 – BL Add MS 40748, Bowes MS III fs 103-4
8 – George Bowes' will, now at the University of York, Borthwick Institute, was proved 12 December 1761. The will, although headed Streatlam, was made at Gibside on 7 February 1750 New Style.
9 – Glamis, Bowes MSS 186 bundle 3. Memorandum Book with marbled cover, 1751
10 – DRO D/St/Box 347/37
11 – DRO D/St/V947 Journals 24 & 29 September 175 p 54. An unsigned and undated record (DRO D/St/Box 305) gives further details of the foundations: 'The Foundation of the Column, stands upon Clay, mix'd with Sand, Large Stones about 6 Feet long at the bottom. The Foundation is now 5F 3 I[nches] within Ground, all of large Stones, and laid in Lime.' On other side of page 'The Columns Foundation'.
12 – Glamis, Bowes MSS Box 186 bundle 3. Memorandum Book with marbled cover
13 – DBL Bowes MSS XXXVI Letter 36
14 – The curious form of the cap of Liberty can also be seen in the caricature of John Wilkes by William Hogarth. The print taken from Hogarth's drawing was published in May 1763. The Gibside Liberty cap is different from Hogarth's in that it turns outwards at the rim, while Hogarth's version is straight.
15 – Reinhold R. Angerstein, from the Journal of his travels in England. 'Resa genons England 1753-55', MS Journal in Jernkontor Library Stockholm, fs 203-4. Angerstein was visiting the Crowley ironworks at Winlaton Mill, just over a mile from Gibside House on the opposite bank of the River Derwent.
16 – Climenson, *Elizabeth Montagu Correspondence 1720 to 1761* Vol. II pp 36-7

17 – Pococke. 'Northern Journeys of Bishop Pococke', Surtees Society 124 (1914) p 240
18 – DRO D/St/991 Cash Accounts 31 August 1754
19 – BL Add MS 40748, Bowes MSS III f 123
20 – DRO D/St/Box 140/90

## Chapter 6: The Chapel

1 – Glamis, Bowes MSS Vol. 39 p 127
2 – Ibid., Vol. 37 p 3
3 – Ibid., Vol. 42 Letter 40
4 – DRO D/St/Box 97
5 – Glamis, Bowes MSS Vol. 8 letter 6
6 – Leach, *James Paine* p 63-6
7 – James Paine, *Plans, Elevations and Sections of Noblemen's and Gentlemen's Houses* Vol. I (1767) p 16
8 – Ibid., Paine p ii
9 – BL Add MS 40748, Bowes MSS III f 123
10 – DRO D/St/V993 Cash Accounts 23 November 1759
11 – Ibid., V994 12 August 1763
12 – DRO D/St/V953 Journals 19 July 1765 p 221
13 – DRO D/St/V994 Cash Accounts 30 August 1765
14 – DRO D/St/V973A Ledgers 31 December 1765 p 127
15 – DRO D/St/V983 23 March 1768 p 28
16 – Leach, *James Paine* p 147
17 – DRO D/St/Box 316. Ralph Pattisson, the Architect to the Fabric of Gibside Chapel, says that these lights were of two types, half being rectangular and 6 or 8 inches by 12 inches, and the others being about 6 to 8 inches square. Great care had been used to cut these lights in the most advantageous way. It is not easy to give precise measurements as they are difficult of access.
18 – *Monthly Chronicle* Vol. III (1889) p 391
19 – Ackerman, *Palladio* 2nd ed. pp 19-29
20 – Ware's *Palladio* II Chapter XVI p 53
21 – Paine, *Plans* I (1767) p ii
22 – Ackerman, *Palladio* p 127
23 – Ibid., p 137
24 – Stillman, *Church Architecture* p 104
25 – The map of the first Western Wagon-way of 1712 (GPL CK/5 183) shows the village of Gibside situated in the east of the estate.
26 – Harris, *The Artist and the country House* p 196
27 – Hussey, *English Gardens* pp 128-9
28 – Stillman, *Church Architecture* p 104
29 – DRO D/St/V983 Journals March 1768 p 30
30 – DRO D/St/V995 Cash Accounts 31 October and 9 November 1775

## Chapter 7: The Most Intelligent Female Botanist

1 – DRO D/St/Box 185/1. A comment written on this document says that it is by William Leaton, an agent of the Gibside Estate and it was made shortly after George Bowes' death.
2 – Mary Eleanor's *Confessions* about her flirtations and later liaisons were written for her rascally second husband and were not meant for publication. He published them without her consent as part of his campaign to prevent her suing for divorce, and regaining control of her property at Gibside and elsewhere.
3 – Climenson, *Elizabeth Montagu Correspondence* 1720-61 Vol. II p 203
4 – Dobrée, Letters of 4th Earl of Chesterfield, Vol.V, no. 1878 p 2006
5 – Ibid., Vol. VI no. 2437 p 2744
6 – Ibid., Vol. VI no. 2480 pp 2795-6
7 – Toynbee & Whibley, *Correspondence of Thomas Gray* Vol. III no. 541 p 973
8 – Ibid., no. 525 p 1135
9 – Sykes, *Local Records*, Vol. I (1883) pp 270-1
10 – DRO D/St/V995 Cash Accounts 29 February 1772
11 – DRO D/St/V995 Cash Accounts 1 October 1772
12 – Ibid., 5 April 1773
13 – Ibid., 23 July 1773
14 – Ibid., 14 October 1773
15 – DRO D/St/V955 Journals 22 November 1774 p 54
16 – DRO D/St/V995 Cash Accounts 31 December 1775. Richard Stephenson was buried in the churchyard of St. Mary's Church, Whickham in the same grave as his father, also Richard Stephenson, agent to the Gibside Estate.

17 – Ibid., 30 April 1775
18 – Foot, *The Lives of Andrew Robinson Bowes Esq. and the Countess of Strathmore* (1810) p 13
19 – Ibid., pp 11-12
20 – Ibid., p 13
21 – Ibid., pp 5-6
22 – HMC *Carlisle* p 319
23 – Foot, *The Lives of Andrew Robinson Bowes* p 60
24 – Namier and Brook, *The House of Commons* Vol. II p 107
25 – DRO D/St/V996 Cash Accounts 28 August 1779
26 – Arnold, *The Unhappy Countess* p 106

## Chapter 8: A Careful Steward

1 – NLS MS 1080 p 6
2 – DRO D/St/997 Cash Accounts 8 March 1791
3 – NCRO Delaval MSS 2 DE 39/13/16
4 – NCRO DELAVAL MSS 2 DE 39/25/9 26 September 1800
5 – DRO D/St/V1526 House-Building Account 18 January 1808
6 – Thomas, 'Notes on Ford Castle' *Proceedings of Society of Antiquaries of Newcastle* (2nd series) V no. 7 (1891) p 63
7 – DRO D/St/998 Cash Accounts Ralph Brown, upholsterer's bill 22 May 1798
8 – DRO D/St/V981 Ledgers 1 October 1816 p 6 contra and p 7
9 – Summerson, *Architecture in Britain 1530-1830* 7th ed. p 479

## Chapter 9: The Absentee Landlord

1 – D/St/E5/21(1)
2 – Ibid.
3 – DRO D/St/V408 John Bowes' Memorandum Book
4 – Excavations made by Harry Beamish, the National Trust Archaeologist, from January to September 1989, have still not fully explained the use of the stage and its surrounding walls.
5 – Although the new lodges were not shown on the first Ordnance Survey map of Whickham, surveyed in 1857, they were shown on the 2nd edition revised about 1895.
6 – D/St/E5/3/10. Corrugated iron was first introduced in 1828 by R. Walter of Rotherham as recorded by Ronald Tylcote in *A History of Metallurgy*, (2nd ed. 1992) p 153. I am grateful to Stafford Linsley for this reference.
7 – DRO D/St/V408 John Bowes' Memorandum Book

## Chapter 10: The Legacy of John Bowes

1 – BL Add Ms 47030 (Egmont Papers) fs 156-59. Quoted by Willis, *Bridgeman* p 111
2 – Paine, *Plans, Sections, Elevations*, Vol. I (1767) p 19. Text to pl LXIX

# BIBLIOGRAPHY

Books referred to in the Notes
Asterisks denote particularly useful books

Ackerman, James S. *Palladio*. The Architect and Society Series. 2nd ed. Harmondsworth: Penguin Books, 1976

Arnold, Ralph **The Unhappy Countess and her Grandson John Bowes*. London: John Constable, 1957

Beard, Geoffrey *Decorative Plasterwork in Great Britain*. London: Phaidon, 1975

Bowes, Mary Eleanor Countess of Strathmore *The Confessions of the Countess of Strathmore written by herself...* London: Printed for W. Locke, 1793

Climenson, Emily J. ed. *Elizabeth Montagu the Queen of the Blue-Stockings, Her Correspondence from 1720-1761*. 2 Vols. London: John Murray, 1906

Colvin, Howard *A Biographical Dictionary of British Architects 1600-1840*. 2nd ed. London: John Murray, 1978

Dobrée, Bonamy ed. *The Letters of Philip Dormer Stanhope 4th Earl of Chesterfield*. 6 Vols. King's Printers, 1932

Foot, Jesse *The Lives of Andrew Robinson Bowes, Esq., and the Countess of Strathmore*. London: Becket and Porter and Sharwood, Neely, and Jones, [1810]

Friedman, Terry *James Gibbs*. Studies in British Art Series. New Haven and London: Yale University Press, 1984

Halsband, Robert ed. *The Complete Letters of Lady Mary Wortley Montagu*. 3 Vols. Oxford, Clarendon Press, 1965-1967

Halsband, Robert *The Life of Lady Mary Wortley Montagu*. Oxford: Clarendon Press, 1956

Historic Manuscripts Commission 15th Report, Appendix Part VI. *The Manuscripts of the Earl of Carlisle, preserved at Castle Howard*. London: HMSO, 1897

Hughes, Edward **North Country Life in the Eighteenth Century*. London: Oxford University Press, 1952

Hussey, Christopher **English Gardens and Landscapes 1700-1750*. London: Country Life, 1967

Leach, Peter *James Paine*. Studies in Architecture Series. London: Zwemmer, 1988

*Monthly Chronicle of North-Country Lore and Legend*. Vol. 3. Newcastle upon Tyne: W. Scott, 1889

Namier, Sir Lewis and Brooke, John *The House of Commons 1754-1790*. The History of Parliament. 2 Vols. London: HMSO, 1964

Paine, James *Plans, Elevations and Sections of Noblemen and Gentlemen's Houses* ... 2 Vols. London: published by Author, 1767-1783

Palladio, Andrea *The Four Books of Andrea Palladio's Architecture*. London: Isaac Ware, 1738. Reprinted New York: Dover Publications, 1965

Pococke, Richard 'Northern Journies of Bishop Pococke' in *North Country Diaries II*. Surtees Society 124 (1914). Durham: Andrews & Co. 1915, pp 199-252

Røstvig, Maren-Sofie *The Happy Man. Studies in the Metamorphoses of Classical Ideal*. Vol. 2 1700-1760. 2nd ed. Oslo: Universitetsforlaget; New York: Humanities Press, 1971

Sedgwick, Romney *The House of Commons 1715-1754*. The History of Parliament, 2 Vols. London: HMSO, 1970

Summerson, John *Architecture in Britain 1530-1830*. The Pelican, History of Art. 7th ed. [Harmondsworth]: Penguin Books, 1983

Surtees, Robert **History and Antiquities of the County Palatine of Durham*. 4 Vols. London: Nichols, Son & Bentley, Bentley: 1816-1840. Reprinted Wakefield: EP Publishing, 1972

Sykes, John *Local Records: or Historical Register of Remarkable Events*. 3 Vols. Newcastle: John Sykes, 1833. Reprinted by T. Fordyce, 1865-67

Toynbee, Paget and Whibley, Leonard eds. *Correspondence of Thomas Gray*. 3 Vols. Oxford: Clarendon Press, 1933

Tylecote, Ronald F. *A History of Metallurgy*. 2nd ed. London, Institute of Metals, 1992

Willis, Peter *Charles Bridgeman and the English Landscape Garden*. Studies in Architecture Series. London: Zwemmer, 1977

Theses and Articles in Periodicals

Brogden, Wiliam Alvis 'Stephen Switzer and Garden Design in Britain in the Early 18th Century' 2 Vols. PhD Thesis, University of Edinburgh, 1973

Fewster, J.M. 'The Politics and Administration of the Borough of Morpeth in the later 18th Century'. PhD Thesis, University of Durham, King's College, Newcastle upon Tyne, 1960

Leach, Peter *'The Architecture of Daniel Garrett' *Country Life* 156
I 'Designs from a Practical Man' (12 September 1974) p 694-7
II 'A Pioneeer of Rococo Decoration' (19 September 1974) p 766-9
III 'In the Gothic Vein' (26 September 1974) p 834-7

Louw, Hentie J. 'The Origin and Development of the Sash-window in the 17th and 18th Centuries, with specific reference to England'. D. Phil. Thesis, University of Oxford, 1981

*Proceedings of the Society of Antiquaries of Newcastle upon Tyne* 2nd series, II, no. 23 (1886)

Rowan, Alistair 'Gothic Restoration at Raby Castle'. *Architectural History* 15 (1972) pp 23-50

Stillman, Damie 'Church Architecture in Neo-Classical England' *Journal of the Society of Architectural Historians* 38, no. 2 (May 1979) pp 103-119

Thomas, Walter B. 'Notes on Ford Castle', *Proceedings of the Society of Antiquaries of Newcastle* 2nd Series V no. 7 (1891) p 63

Wills, Margaret 'One of its kind. The Newcastle Infirmary', *Country Life* 185 (10 October 1991) p 124

## FURTHER READING

In addition to items marked with an asterisk, the following books give useful further reading:

Hardy, John E. *John Bowes and the Bowes Museum.* Bishop Auckland: The Author, 1970

Robinson, John Martin *Georgian Model Farms. A Study of the Decorative Model Farm Buildings in the Age of Improvement.* 1700-1846. Oxford: Clarendon Press, 1983

Switzer, Stephen *Ichnographia Rustica.* 3 Vols. London: D. Browne, 1718. Reprinted Garland Publishing, 1982

# INDEX

# PUBLICATIONS OF THE NEWCASTLE SOCIETY OF ANTIQUARIES

The following publications of the Society may be obtained by writing to the Publications Section, The Society of Antiquaries of Newcastle upon Tyne, The Black Gate, Castle Garth, Newcastle upon Tyne NE1 1RQ with the appropriate payment:

ST. WILFRID'S CRYPTS AT RIPON AND HEXHAM: a Visitors' Guide
by Richard Bailey, at £2.95 each.

RECORD SERIES:
I THE NORTHUMBERLAND LAY SUBSIDY ROLL OF 1296;
editor C. M. Fraser, at £6.00 each.
II MONOPOLY OF THE TYNE 1650-58;
editor R. Howell jnr, at £6.00 each.
III THE ACCOUNTS OF THE CHAMBERLAINS OF NEWCASTLE UPON TYNE 1508-1511; editor C. M. Fraser, at £15.00 each.

MONOGRAPH SERIES:
II CATALOGUE OF SMALL FINDS FROM SOUTH SHIELDS ROMAN FORT
by L. Allason-Jones and R. F. Miket at £30.00 each.
III THE ORIGINS OF NEWCASTLE QUAYSIDE
by C. F. O'Brien and others, at £12.50 each.
IV EXCAVATIONS AT SOUTH SHIELDS ROMAN FORT
Volume I, by Paul Bidwell and Stephen Speak, at £35.00 each.

REPRINTS from *Archaeologia Aeliana:*
I ASPECTS OF THE ANGLO-NORMAN DESIGN OF DURHAM CATHEDRAL
by Ian Curry, at £2.95 each.
II NEWCASTLE UPON TYNE'S *THEATRES ROYAL* 1788-1870
by Ken Robinson, at £2.95 each.
III WHISKY SMUGGLING ON THE BORDER
by John Philipson, at £2.95 each.

BUILDINGS OF NEWCASTLE
I THE COOPERAGE 32-34 The Close, a timber framed building in Newcastle upon Tyne,
by David Heslop and Laurence Truman, at £2.50 each.

Cheques payable to *The Society of Antiquaries of Newcastle upon Tyne*. Prices given are post free but are subject to revision.